HELPING YOUR TEEN-AGE STUDENT

What Parents Can Do to Improve Reading and Study Skills

MARVIN COHN, Ph.D.

E. P. DUTTON • NEW YORK

For information contact: E.P. Dutton, 2 Park Avenue, New York, N.Y. 10016

Library of Congress Cataloging in Publication Data

Cohn, Marvin.   Helping your teen-age student.

1. Reading.   2. Books and reading for youth.   3. Study, Method of.
4. Report writing. I. Title. LB1050.C573 1979   373.1'3'02813   79-9767

ISBN: 0-525-93065-5

Published simultaneously in Canada by Clarke, Irwin & Company Limited, Toronto and Vancouver

Designed by Barbara Huntley

10 9 8 7 6 5 4 3 2 1

First Edition

To my wife

CONTENTS

PREFACE

A book such as this one clearly represents the distillation of the experience, judgment, and expertise of many people. I am grateful to all of them. Eleanor and George Abend are dear friends who were particularly generous with their careful consideration and many suggestions. Among the other people who have read portions of the manuscript and have made helpful comments and suggestions have been James Ace, Mildred Carter, Dr. Irwin Lesser, Shirley Maslow, Dolores Norman, Pearl Rabinowitz, Dr. Lorraine Schottenfeld, Dr. Ernest Siegel, and Harold Weller. I hope I have included all of them. Many others generously offered their help. Mrs. Gloria Regan struggled through my handwriting to type the manuscript.

People who perhaps unwittingly played a role in shaping this book through their influences on my education and career include Dr. Gerald G. Glass, Dr. Josephine Piekarz-Ives, and Dr. Nila B. Smith. I should like to thank the many staff members and children with whom I have worked at the Adelphi University Reading and Learning Disability Center. I have learned from all of them.

I know that authors conventionally pay tribute to their wives, and the help they have given. I doubt that other authors have had the kind of concerned and balanced thoughtfulness that my wife, Helen, has put into the reading of the manuscript. Her helpful comments resulted in many improvements of this book.

I have had to use pronouns in writing about imaginary pupils and teachers. Both can be of either sex, of course, but it is inconvenient and clumsy to write both a male and female pronoun each time. I have solved the problem by assuming that the teacher is female and the pupil is male.

HELPING YOUR TEEN-AGE STUDENT

CHAPTER 1

Is this book for you?

Have you ever noticed those strange noises at report card and teacher conference times? You are hearing the sound of battle flags being raised and snapping in the wind. At these times when birds cock their heads to one side, listen, and fly away hurriedly, I suspect they are leaving because they hear parents' blood pressures rising.

Perhaps you try to head off school problems before they begin by starting on them early in the term. You want to get close to your child, show him you're interested, and offer your help if he's in trouble. So you ask:

"What did you do in school today?"

"Nothin'."

"Hm, well what did you study in English?"

"The Grapes of Wrath." (Ah! Good, that was one of your favorite books!) "What an awful book! I'm never going to eat grapes again."

"And what happened in math?"

(Enthusiastically) "We had a substitute today, and boy did we drive *her* up the wall!"

"Well, what about social studies?"

"Oh, that's boring too. We never understand what he's talking about. Say, how did the Boston Red Sox do today?"

I don't know how the Red Sox did, but you just struck out—

all your fine hopes and intentions were swept aside with the kind of abrupt rejection that leads directly to exploding tempers. Somehow a situation that started out to be giving and affectionate suddenly got turned around and became angry and uncomfortable.

Of course, we don't all engage in pitched battles with children about their schoolwork. However, some of us know, while many others only suspect and worry that our junior or senior high school youngster ought to be doing better in school.

Does Your Child Have a Problem?

Problems can appear in many ways. Perhaps for years teachers have been saying that this youngster's schoolwork is satisfactory, but he should be doing better. Perhaps the grades are acceptable, or even very good, but the youngster works so hard to get them and is under such strain that he doesn't feel good about what he's doing. On the other hand, his work may be passing even though he claims that he rarely has homework— "I did it all in study hall"—or never spends more than fifteen minutes doing it.

Some parents or teachers feel that there is too big a discrepancy between the way a youngster functions in school and the way he functions outside of it. Or sometimes we see him doing much better in difficult school subjects than in easy ones. Or we remember that he did well in school up to a certain grade, but nose-dived after that.

Sometimes the youngster's work hasn't been satisfactory for a while, and he's getting discouraged. Or he's been getting easy things wrong for too long a time. Perhaps he's having so hard a time that he's thinking of leaving school as soon as he can, instead of going on to further education.

What Have You Done About It Up to Now?

Are your usual efforts to help largely suggestions like "Why don't you spend more time on it?" or "Go over it once more!" or "Study harder!"? You say those things because you want to help, and because you don't know what else to say. Those statements, however, assume that the student really knows what to do, but just doesn't spend enough time doing it. Suppose the student doesn't know what to do and is using the wrong techniques? Will spending more time doing the wrong things really help him? There you are—a student who wants to do better and an adult who wants to help, but neither of you knows how to go about it. If I've just described your situation, relax. This book was written to help both of you.

Or are you one of those parents who says "He (or she) just doesn't care. He could do better, but it just doesn't matter to him." I don't think that's true, although it often looks as if it is. I always ask students who come to the Adelphi University Reading and Learning Disability Center for testing, "What do you think your biggest school problem is?" Many of them say, "The work is boring." Many others say, "I don't pay much attention to school because I'm going to work at a job that doesn't need it." It always turns out that those children have serious reading skill problems. So although I always listen respectfully, I never start a debate about those comments. They're smoke screens put up by the kids to explain why they aren't doing well—it hurts less that way. After all, can such students be anything but bored if they don't understand the material? If you had long-standing problems with schoolwork, would you choose a job that exposed your weaknesses?

Those students have the cart before the horse. Their boredom with schoolwork and interest in other areas are the *result* of poor schoolwork, not the *cause* of it. And poor schoolwork often comes from poor skills. So I don't debate their "reasons" with them. We simply get right to work improving their skills, and before long they understand better, their schoolwork becomes more interesting, and their marks improve. This book will show you how to help this problem solve itself.

Or, seeing that the student is unwilling to spend time at schoolwork, have you decided that laziness is the problem? Again, the so-called laziness is an end result, not a cause. We see it because the student has already decided that more effort is too painful or won't really help. Lazy people are unwilling to put out effort for anything. If someone suggests playing baseball, or going for an ice-cream soda, is this person still slow-moving and unwilling? I suspect that real laziness doesn't exist. People appear to be lazy when they dread the thing they have to do. When you get at the cause of the problem, which I'll help you to do, the "laziness" will disappear.

But Can You Really Do Anything About It?

Many parents are concerned, but they're discouraged. For one thing, often these problems have been going on for years, with no improvement. For another, most parents are not teachers and don't know how to help. And some others have tried to help, with poor or disastrous results.

The adult begins to feel that the student is letting him down. The student senses the adult's disappointment and feels that the adult isn't on his side. That only increases his feelings of failure and his anger at himself, the adult, and the school. As angry people, they can't work together in a positive way. The combination is deadly—the direct opposite of what they both want.

Finally, many people wonder if trying to help the child isn't harmful. After all, it openly tells the child that something is wrong, and may therefore damage the child's self-image even further. Let's consider these points one by one.

You Can Help Effectively!

For years, many teachers have worked with children who have long-term reading and study problems. Our experience shows that most of them can improve, sometimes dramatically, provided they get the right kind of help. Sometimes the most hopeless, difficult-looking situations are easier than they look if you take the correct approach.

Let me tell you about a youngster we worked with recently. Steve was fifteen and a student, of sorts, at a school for disturbed children. His problems were far more severe than the ones your youngster faces.

I walked down to the waiting room, never having met Steve. Before I got there, I looked ahead and saw only one youngster his age. He stood in a half-crouch, with his back to the wall, slamming his hand into the wall at a slow, steady pace. I stopped in the hallway, thinking, "That must be Steve. Is he really that upset about having to read? If so, it will be very hard, maybe impossible for us to help him. But suppose he's a manipulative person? Maybe this is a pose, designed to make us feel sorry for him, so that we won't ask him to struggle to learn to read. If so, it has apparently worked well up to now, because according to his records he's a very poor reader. Are his pain and fear real, or is this just a pose?" I decided to stay where I was in the hall and observe him for a minute or two. I noticed that although his head remained down, his eyes turned toward each adult who walked into the waiting room. He was not wrapped up in his own feelings—he was trying to see if his behavior was affecting *us*. Then it *was* a pose. Knowing that, we worked with him for over a year. His disruptive behavior, which was designed to get us to make fewer demands on him, gradually decreased when he saw it didn't work. In addition, since we were teaching him to read more effectively, the "acting" became neither useful nor necessary. We've helped in many cases such as Steve's, so there's a very good chance we can help you with your youngster too.

However, you may feel that you're not the right person to provide that kind of help because you're not a teacher. That may not be as important as you think. After all, most secondary school teachers teach a particular subject, such as English or math. Relatively few of them are trained to deal with long-term reading problems. And you have a number of strengths they may lack. The fact that you're reading this book shows that you're concerned and want to help. You've known this youngster much longer than his teachers have, probably since he was born. In that case, you understand what he's doing now compared to what he could do before. Further, while a good teacher can learn a lot about a child during forty-five minute periods in, let's say, social studies, you as a parent or other adult have observed him in that and many other activities as well. This gives you a much more complete picture. Last, if you try to help this child, you will probably work with him in a one-to-one situation. All of your attention and corrective work are devoted to him alone. You don't have to be concerned about meeting the needs of the other twenty-five or thirty children in the class. The teacher would love to trade places with *you* in some ways.

Of course, teachers know how to teach subject matter and skills. But that's just why this book was written. It's designed to give you some of that know-how in the following ways:

1. You will probably feel calmer when you see that many other children have the same difficulties that your child does. If they didn't, there would have been no need to write this book.

2. The school difficulties and complaints we hear are frequently not what they appear to be. This book will help you to zero in on what the underlying difficulties *really* are.

3. Once you accurately identify those difficulties, you'll be in a much better position to help your child by following our suggestions to correct these problems.

You may still be concerned that trying to help may damage the student's self-image because it implies that he isn't competent. However, the child usually already knows that he is in difficulty. The attitude with which you introduce and discuss the problem is as important as the problem itself. Your approach should show that you feel he is worth helping and have faith in his ability to succeed. In any case, the problems that damage his self-esteem won't go away by themselves. They will only go away if he gets effective help, so why not try to provide him with it?

Is It Too Late?

Every once in a while, as I walk across the campus, a young man or woman will stop me and ask, "Do you remember me?" He or she usually reminds me that he was in my class at the clinic some years ago. When I ask what he's doing now, he tells me he is a student at the university. Some of them are working for master's degrees or doctorates. Yet our clinic doesn't attract students with temporary or minor problems who only need a bit of tutoring in an individual subject. We work almost exclusively with pupils whose marks are low or failing and who have major problems in reading or studying.

Sometimes, when I talked to parents about the work their children were doing in the clinic, they'd say they could tell what kind of work was going on. They'd guess that I'd been teaching their children how to find a main idea, or to research and write a report, because they had seen so much improvement in those areas. Sometimes, of course, they were right, but not always. Sometimes I had only worked with the youngster at much more basic, low-level skills. What happened? Those kids began to see that they could improve. That encouraged some of them to relax and use more of their mental energy doing some of the things they had always avoided before. Their work even began to improve in areas in which I was not helping them.

This carry-over effect didn't happen to all the youngsters I worked with. Most kids with a history of long-term difficulty don't quickly become self-starters who improve in other skills on their own. A kid has to have pretty good feelings about himself before that will happen, and few poor students feel that way. But we do see steady improvement, and eventually the youngster becomes more independent and competent.

With all of these considerations in mind, I have tried to organize the book in a way that I believe will be most helpful to you. Please go back and look at the table of contents now. Each chapter title is a remark or observation that I have heard many children and/or their parents make. Perhaps some of these statements will sound familiar to you. As you read the book, pay special attention to those chapters. The book will give you new insights into what your child's problem really is, and will suggest corrective measures to help solve the problem. You may also locate techniques that you don't need to use now, but that you will need in a month or two.

A good way to approach this book is to read it once, noticing which parts of it describe your youngster's difficulties. Pay special attention to those sections that deal with attitudes—yours and your child's. The attitudes with which you tackle a job are as important as the work itself—sometimes more important. Then reread those parts that deal with the problems your youngster has, and think about them carefully. If a youngster has a number of problems, sometimes one or more of them has to be corrected before the others. For example, a youngster has to learn how to understand easy material before he learns how to understand difficult material. So establish your priorities carefully when you pick the problems you plan to correct. Then carefully reread the area or areas you plan to work on first.

CHAPTER 2

Getting ready to help

Perhaps you seriously question whether you can help your youngster because your past attempts didn't work out well. If that's so, probably a big part of the problem had to do with attitudes. So before I show you how to recognize and correct specific learning problems, let's look at the attitudes that parents and children have toward schoolwork and schools.

What are your own attitudes toward school and your child's activities in it? Certainly you want your child to do well in school, or you wouldn't be reading this book. However, there is more to it than that. Most people have more than one attitude toward school. These other attitudes come from their own past experiences as students, among other things. Here is a short questionnaire to help you discover what some of your attitudes are.

How did you feel about the time you spent as a student?
   a. Enjoyed it
   b. Tolerated it
   c. Felt uncomfortable

Is your child aware of how you felt about school?

Do you feel that the things you learned in school helped you in later life?

Is your child aware of those feelings?

When is your child absent from school?
  a. Only when he's really sick, or for rare family emergencies
  b. Occasionally for chores and/or family vacations
  c. Occasionally for other reasons too

How do you feel when you visit your child's school?
  a. Comfortable
  b. Defensive
  c. Angry

How often do you visit your child's school, and for what purposes?

If your child asks for help with his homework, are you
  a. Glad to help?
  b. Concerned you won't know what to do?
  c. Annoyed?

How often are education and its goals discussed at home?
  a. Never
  b. Rarely
  c. Occasionally

How does your child hear you talk about his school?
  a. Usually positively
  b. As often positively as negatively
  c. Usually negatively

How do you regard teachers?
  a. Feel they are generally concerned about their students' education
  b. Judge them on an individual basis
  c. Feel they're more concerned with their own interests than their pupils'

When your child describes a problem with a teacher, do you
  a. Ask the teacher how she sees the problem?
  b. Write a letter or telephone to complain to the teacher?
  c. Go directly to an administrator to complain?

Should teaching methods be dependent on
  a. Teacher choice?
  b. Parental choice?

c. Student choice?

d. All three?

Do you privately wish the school wouldn't bother you with notices about your child's lateness, skipping classes, etc.?

Do you believe that school achievement and behavior problems should be dealt with in school and not at home?

Perhaps the questionnaire has reminded you of difficulties you had when you were a student. If so, it may be hard for you to look at your child's school problems without your own earlier feelings getting aroused. However, your child's school problems are his own, not yours. If you are careful, your attitudes can make things easier for him, but remember, they are still his problems.

How do parents talk about education at home? There is a wave of negative feeling about schools and teachers in our country today. From time to time people talk about a teacher, a teaching method, or some school policy that they don't like. Many people feel that the schools are too permissive. Others feel that schools demand either too little or too much work from their students. Some worry about declining achievement scores. People express negative opinions when the local education budget and the school board members come up for votes, and when teachers' contracts come up for renewal.

Don't misunderstand me. People should and do have the right to express their opinions. However, it's easier to blame than to praise. Parents voice their criticisms and take it for granted that the child knows that, in spite of the criticism, they feel that education is important and necessary. They want their children to do well in school. They mean to object only to some of the things the school is doing. However, if these negative remarks are most (or all) of what is said about education, the children who hear them draw the conclusion that education is not respected and desirable. Many children begin to feel that what the schools ask them to do is not important or worth the effort. Later they are surprised when their parents tell them they haven't worked hard enough at school.

Of course there are other influences that affect our attitudes to education. But the home itself is a very important influence, *and one that we can do something about.* By all means take an interest in your child's education. That's one way of showing him you think it's important. Let your child hear you criticize the school if you want to, but recognize that that imposes another responsibility on you each time you do it. There are two separate issues here: First, the school wants the student to learn. So do you. Second, the school has certain ways of achieving that result. Make the difference between the relative importance of each of these issues clear to your child. The most important one is the first, which you wholeheartedly support. You may not always like the way the school functions, but the child should not interpret that to mean that the importance of good achievement is lessened in any way.

If you're concerned that this is what has happened, start to undo the damage. Plan to have a heart-to-heart talk about it as soon as the time is right. Explain that your previous comments about school were restricted to individual situations, but that you regard learning itself as very important, and that you want your child to do his best to get a good education. Be alert to reinforce this impression from time to time.

When a child comes home with a complaint, it's very easy to assume that the school is wrong. This amounts to prejudgment, which is risky. Put yourself in the teacher's shoes. Suppose that a student brings a complaint about you to his parent. How do you want to be treated at this point? Should the parent, without further investigation, decide that the complaint is justified? Or should the parent say: "This is my child's version of what happened. Let's hear the other person's version too. Then I'll be in a better position to know what is going on." Nobody is right every time he makes a complaint.

When you hear a complaint, start by respecting both sides. Protect yourself against the possibility of misjudging the situation. In a calm and positive way ask the teacher for her view of what happened. You may learn that your child was honestly mistaken or unaware of some aspect of what was going on. You may learn something that explains the problem or changes the focus of it. One teacher I know recently faced a furious parent who complained that her youngster had stayed up to all hours to do the previous day's assignment. It turned out that the assignment had been given four weeks earlier, but the pupil hadn't done anything about it until the last day.

Sometimes, of course, talking to the school reveals that the complaint is justified. The parent who has been calm and rational makes it easier for the school to correct the problem. Sometimes the school feels it can't or won't correct it, and you and the child are stuck with it. I think this happens rarely, but it does happen. In that case, support your child, but since you also believe that he needs the best education he can get, support that too. Tell your child that next term's work may be dependent on this term's. This term's work will certainly affect his report card. Unfortunately, he is responsible to learn the work whether or not the circumstances are all they might be. You will help him in all the ways you can, because it's important that he learns, no matter how he feels about the school or the teacher.

Sometimes the parent unknowingly takes an attitude that encourages the child to avoid his educational responsibilities. Occasionally when I try to describe the way a child functions, the parent constantly interrupts me. Each weakness is excused by statements that all mean the same thing: It just isn't his fault that he hasn't learned a specific process or body of information. He had a poor teacher in that grade. Or there was too much noise in the classroom. Or, as one mother said to me, "Other children were permitted to make jokes and not do their work, so he joined them. Wouldn't you?" (No.) If his parents maintain this view, the child grows up feeling that the cause of his problem is always outside of himself. Therefore there is no need for *him* to change. This parent is excusing the child's failure to learn.

If on careful consideration you feel that your youngster is in a bind because you have excused his failure to function in the past, start to step back from your earlier behavior. This should be done slowly and carefully. Otherwise your child will feel that you have suddenly withdrawn your understanding and support. Then too, he will be very uncomfortable finding out how hard he has to work. Further, people find it difficult to handle a complete, rapid turnabout in any close relationship. So go slowly. Next time you see he hasn't learned something, or isn't doing well in a class, point out that his report card will reflect *his* work, not his teacher's. Ask him to learn one small part or process now. Offer whatever help and support you can, but insist that he learn it. Gradually, very gradually, step up the proportion of things he must learn in that class.

Is It the Child's Fault?

Many parents feel that their children are to blame for their difficulties with schoolwork. Here are some of the things they say.

1. "It's the child's fault because he sits in front of the television set until it's too late. Then he's too tired or doesn't have enough time to do his homework, so his schoolwork suffers." Many people, when they watch TV, find it hard to take their attention away from it. This causes them to delay doing other things they need to do until sometimes it's too late. (Parents aren't immune to this problem either.) And the TV set's being there makes the temptation enormous—just hit the switch, anytime, for instant pleasure. Before people know it, they've let the TV set control them, instead of their controlling it. That's exactly what this is—a problem in control.

   Unfortunately, it's not as easy as most other control problems. For example, if you like ice cream (or pizza, or whatever) you can't lose control and eat twenty or thirty portions of it at a time. Not only does your body need other foods, but your stomach fills up. You *must* stop. When you watch TV, nothing fills up (in more ways than one, unfortunately). Your body has no signal that forces you to stop. Only your mind can force you to stop, and that's busy paying attention to the TV set.

The problem is that after you start to watch it's harder to make an intelligent decision about when to stop. The right time to make that decision is *before* you start. Sit down and discuss the scheduling problem with your student. The issue is not "How much TV is too much?" The issue is that sensible people learn to control their lives. They first must be sure to do the things they have to do. Then they can do the things they want to do. Young people should be taught to schedule their time, so that they can handle both kinds of things adequately. If this means that they can't watch as much TV as they want to, that kind of situation is no surprise to them. They can't spend as much money as they want to, or eat as much ice cream as they want to either. The younger your child is when you try to get him to think in these terms, the easier the job will be.

2. Many parents feel that their youngster's difficulty with schoolwork arises at least partly from the youngster's doing homework or studying with the TV set or the radio on. Few things divide parents and children more. Parents are absolutely convinced that it's impossible to give full attention to homework "with all that noise going on," and their children are convinced that it doesn't hurt a bit. Some even say that it helps them to concentrate. "Besides, everybody else in my class does it that way." The battle is joined. This problem gets more difficult to solve as the child gets older, so the earlier you work it out, the better off everyone will be. One parent I know asked the child to perform an experiment. The child did his homework for one week with the radio on, and one week with it off. At the end of the two weeks they discussed it. Which way was it easier? If you're lucky, this experiment will help resolve the issue.

3. Parents frequently explain poor schoolwork by accusing their children of not caring or of being lazy. These "explana-

tions" were discussed in Chapter 1. They are not helpful, and rarely, if ever, are they accurate.

4. Some parents, seeing that the usual motivations to do better at school have not succeeded, resort to bribery. One parent told me that when his son recently received a failing grade in Spanish, he offered to buy the boy an expensive pair of ski boots if his grade went up to 90 on the next report card. The boy earned the 90 and received the boots. In the following marking period his grade dropped to 30 again.

The theory behind the bribe is that it gets the child to pull his grades up. When he sees he can get good grades, the parents hope the child will be motivated to continue getting them, and further bribes will be unnecessary. Sometimes the bribe appears to work, sometimes it doesn't. Some children can't improve their grades because they have real skill problems. Others do pull their grades up, but there is no carryover, and the bribing must continue or the grades go down.

There is another, more significant objection to the bribe. Is it right to constantly bribe someone to do something that he or she is normally supposed to do? Do you have to behave that way with your wife or husband? Should the student's achievement be the result of a constant, unending series of bribes? The consistent giving of bribes says: "Don't learn because you need to know the material, or because you ought to develop your own competence by mastering it. Instead, learn because if you do, I'll give you something else you *really* want." We are teaching the child that we think that learning is not as important as some material reward that is arbitrarily and temporarily related to it by us. Would you say to your child: "Stay healthy because if you do I'll give you money for it?" Somewhere, I suspect, there are a few students who occasionally intentionally do poor work so that they can keep the bribes coming. In such cases, the bribe backfires, and encourages the child to slip back into poor grades.

Don't confuse bribes with rewards. It's a nice gesture if, at irregular intervals, a parent surprises a student by giving him a compliment or a small gift in recognition of a job well done. Since the reward is not promised in advance, and the student doesn't expect to receive it, he is not being urged to work for the sake of a gift. Then too, this is a nice way for the parents to show that they think good schoolwork is important and that they appreciate their youngster's performance in it.

5. A few parents, angry over their youngster's failure to achieve adequately, resort to the opposite of bribery, punishment. The parent assumes that the child has let things slide, isn't really bothered by the poor grades, and can do better if he wants to. Those assumptions are usually not true. The child may be in over his head with skills problems he can't do anything about by himself. He may feel the embarrassment of poor grades keenly. If so, when he is in trouble he feels his parent's anger and lack of support even more keenly. In many cases, the student can't do better without help, no matter how hard he tries. Further, punishment misses the boat the same way that bribery does. We want the child to learn because there are things he needs to know, and because if he learns successfully, he will see that he is a competent person. Punishment says: "Learn in order to avoid pain, not to become a better person." Thus, even when it appears to work, punishment introduces its own problems. But it rarely works. Most children know that the punishment is temporary. They can "wait out" their parents.

We have characterized certain attitudes as less than helpful. Many of them ("he's lazy," "he doesn't care," "he watches TV too much," and so forth), focus on an end result instead of the cause of the problem, which is that the child has already given up. This is really a story without villains, so don't waste time looking for them. Instead, as we suggest, make your effort really productive by figuring out (with us) what the learning problems are, and correcting them. You will see that many of the other issues will get better by themselves, and so will your relationship to your child.

Without doubt, many parents present positive attitudes. They make it clear to their child in a variety of ways that education is something to be valued and worked for. They are interested in the subject matter studied in his classes. They go to and even ask for conferences with his teachers, to find out for themselves what his teachers are like and what they think of his schoolwork. They praise him when he does something well or better than he was able to do before. They are supportive and helpful when the youngster needs their help. They are also firm and fair when that's required.

You may be concerned that your past attitudes toward your student and his school may get in the way of his improvement. Here's a simple way to deal with that. After this book helps you to focus on which learning problem he has, sit down with your youngster and try to help him with it. After a few sessions (so that he doesn't have to get used to too many new things at once), tell him you would like to tape record the session, because you want to hear how you come across to him. Wait a day or two to get some distance from the lesson, and then play the tape back to yourself. You will probably get a new awareness of what your attitudes are and how they are expressed. Tape and listen to subsequent lessons too, to see if things are changing. You'll find that your youngster is not the only one who can do better.

CHAPTER 3

"But you just read that word correctly a minute ago!"

Is there anyone more infuriating or difficult to understand than the older child who misreads an easy word that he was taught in the first or second grade? If there is, perhaps it's the youngster who reads a word correctly, only to get it wrong a minute later. Then of course, there is the youngster who does both these things.

These errors make us panicky. We wonder how serious a problem the child must have when he can't even read simple words. Worse yet, if he doesn't read the words properly, how can he conceivably understand the passage?

This problem usually looks a lot worse than it really is. Making word recognition or decoding errors (as teachers call them now) is very common, but it is rarely caused by an inability to decode the words and seldom interferes with the youngster's ability to comprehend. I'm not saying there are no youngsters with decoding problems, but they're not nearly as common as they appear to be.

Looking at Word Recognition Errors

How did you come to suspect that your youngster has decoding problems? If he or she made a number of errors reading aloud to you, you feel positive that the problem exists, because you heard it yourself. You may be right, but there's a good chance that you're not.

I recently tested a charming fourteen-year-old girl. Her parents were both professionals, and very bright. Her mother felt that the girl decoded poorly because whenever she read something aloud she hesitated frequently and made many errors. After her mother left, I gave the girl a decoding test. She also read four long paragraphs to me at her own grade level or higher—all of this without making a single decoding error. Her oral reading was done rapidly, fluently, and with good expression. To top it off, in another test she read several paragraphs and answered 122 multiple-choice questions, getting only two of them wrong. That's the highest proportion of correct answers I've ever seen on this test. Is there any chance at all that she really doesn't know how to decode?

Why did she make mistakes in reading at home? Think about your own experiences for a moment. Weren't your parents often the last ones before whom you could "perform," especially when you weren't sure of yourself? You knew they loved you and wanted so much for you to succeed that even your little failures were painful to them. And I'll bet there were even times when you were so tense about doing well that your performance was weaker than if you'd been calm. If anxiety about performing in some situations is what's causing your youngster's errors, that's usually only temporary. Have you (or others) heard this youngster reading more effectively to friends, or when he was more relaxed, or when he didn't know that you were listening? Did the youngster do well on tests that had to be decoded? If so, the decoding problem is more apparent than real. This emphasizes how important it is to be calm and accepting when your youngster makes an error. One thing is certain— if you get tense and uncomfortable or angry, you're doing the most effective thing you can to rattle your youngster and have him make even more errors.

But what about those youngsters who make many decoding errors all the time, even in the best of circumstances? Aren't they people we need to be concerned about? Perhaps, but not necessarily. Believe it or not, these errors are rarely as serious as they appear to be. We can probably understand them, and what to do about them, if we see what they really are.

In Context or Out?

Were the words read incorrectly from a list, or in meaningful sentences? Often children's ability to recognize and pronounce words correctly is judged by how they decode a list of words. Some reading tests, such as the reading part of the Wide Range Achievement Test, measure word recognition in that way only. That's artificial, and most unfair. Isn't almost all normal reading done in sentences, in a context that makes sense? I have tested thousands of children over the last twenty-five years, and I almost invariably find that the same children recognize the words much better in sentences and paragraphs than they do when these words are decoded from lists. We'll discuss why this is true later in this chapter, but rest assured, it is true.

Which Words Were Missed?

If the child made errors in reading sentences, what kinds of words were misread? Were they words that were easy to sound out, such as *ring* or *came?* Were the errors made on common endings *(s, es, ed, ing)?* Did the youngster miss a number of everyday, small words *(a, the, this, that,* and the like) but get the bigger, harder words right? If these were the only kinds of "errors" made, relax. Your child knows how to read those words correctly. He was probably more interested in attending to the meaning than in getting the decoding exactly right. Don't you occasionally make such "errors" too?

Sometimes the decoding errors appear in other places. If you use the technique for recording errors that's discussed later in this chapter, you may find a pattern. For example, the author has written "ham and cheese," and the student reads "ham and eggs." The student read the begining of the phrase and then completed it the way he thought it would be. He simply jumped the gun. It's clear that these errors don't come from a lack of knowledge of phonics. What, if anything, you do about it depends on what the student does after he makes the error.

If the student usually corrects himself, you needn't do anything about it. If the student's error doesn't make sense in the context, and the student doesn't correct himself, read Chapter 4. That's a different kind of problem. Suppose the student's errors make sense, and he doesn't correct himself. Ask him about the author's meaning in several of these decoding slips. You want to find out if he usually knows the right information, but just doesn't go back to change what he said. If he doesn't know what the author said, show him that his problem is a tendency to complete the phrase before he has read it, and ask him to pay some attention to this problem when he reads. An occasional reminder (from you) can be helpful too.

Other errors appear to be more serious. Are they? Did they involve words with letters that don't take the same sound they usually do (su*b*tle, fa*ca*de, *chaos*)? Were they words with letters that are consistently pronounced in one way, but are rarely seen in those combinations (face*tious,* uni*que,* effi*cient*)? These errors tell us that the youngster is unfamiliar with some unusual letter combinations, not that he's weak in decoding.

Sometimes vocabulary difficulties masquerade as decoding problems. On a test I use almost daily, the children have to decode the word *blunt,* which many of them encounter for the first time. It's an easy word to decode because it consists of the common combinations *bl* and *unt,* which are pronounced just as expected. But when some of the children silently decode *blunt* correctly, they feel that can't be right because they never heard the word before. So they hesitate, and usually say "bunt" instead. That *appears* to be a problem in not knowing what sound to make for the letters *bl,* but it would be wasteful to spend time teaching those children what sound *bl* represents, since they already know that. Their error comes from another source altogether. In any case, getting a word wrong often occurs when a child has figured it out correctly, but it turns out to be unfamiliar.

All the many kinds of errors we've talked about so far occur *in spite of* an adequate knowledge of decoding. But perhaps your youngster really doesn't know what sounds to make for many letters. I think that's quite rare for secondary school children, but here's how to find out if that's the problem.

Getting the Information You Need

Select a three-hundred-word passage from your child's social studies book. You will need to make a typed or handwritten copy of the passage. Be sure your copy leaves enough space between the lines for you to record your reader's errors. (If you can't get the social studies book, use an article from a newspaper, or even a passage from this book.) Select a passage that your youngster hasn't read before. If he seems to be very nervous about it, let him look it over for a minute or two.

It's a good idea to tell your youngster what he'll be doing. If the youngster is tense and you start this diagnostic exercise (please don't call it a test, for obvious reasons) without telling him anything about it, his anxiety may know no bounds simply because, like most people, he fears most what he knows least about. So tell him that he'll be reading aloud, and that it will just take a few minutes. He will usually be a lot less anxious. However, it's not a good idea to tell him that the exercise is designed to tell you how well he recognizes words. That may make him tense. You want him to perform just as he normally does.

While the youngster reads the passage aloud, follow along on your copy. If he omits a word, cross it out. When he adds a word, write it in above the line, showing exactly where he added it. If he misreads a word, write it in above the original word. Be sure to indicate exactly how he said it. If he makes a mistake, but corrects it himself, do not count it as an error. When he finishes, jot down a few words that describe his reading. Probably your written comment will include one or more of these: "moderate pace," "too fast," "too slow," "hesitant," "doesn't stop for punctuation," "expression good."

Now that you've got a group of errors to look at, here are some examples of what you are likely to find. The words that were misread are underlined.

DECODING—DIAGNOSTIC SAMPLE 1

Text, line 1:   Fred drove the car down the <u>road</u>.

Student read: Fred drove the car down the <u>street</u>.

Text, line 2:   He was not <u>exactly</u> sure of the directions.

Student read: He was not <u>excited</u> sure [and then, correcting himself] exactly sure of the directions.

Text, line 3:   "<u>Somehow</u>," he thought, "I must find <u>that</u> old refectory."

Student read: "<u>Somewhere</u>," he thought, "I must find <u>this</u> old refectory."

Let's look at these errors. In line 1, the reader substituted *street* for *road*. In line 2 he substituted *excited* for *exactly,* and in line 3 *Somewhere* for *Somehow,* and *this* for *that*. What is particularly interesting about these errors is that the student misread phonically regular (easy to read correctly), very common words. At the same time he read correctly much more difficult and unusual words, such as *thought* and *refectory*. If he can read the more difficult words, he must be able to read the easier ones. We have already explained why people make such errors.

Remember however, that although decoding errors were made, none of them changed the author's meaning. And following up the question of meaning, let's look at the error in line 2. Here the reader said "excited," but apparently the word *sure,* coming immediately afterward, signaled the possibility of an error. So the reader went back—independently—and read the word *exactly* correctly. In other words, this reader was guided by his careful search for the author's meaning. Though he makes word-recognition errors, he corrects them if they change the author's meaning. Since the only point of accurate word recognition is to enable the reader to get the meaning, this youngster has no significant word-recognition problem. (And I am positive that if you asked the same reader to try again the words he missed before, he would get them right the second time.)

DECODING—DIAGNOSTIC SAMPLE 2

Text, line 1:   He <u>tried</u> his <u>skeleton</u> keys on the door.
Student read: He <u>tired</u> his <u>skillful</u> keys on the door.

Text, line 2:   He worked <u>hurriedly</u>, <u>afraid</u> that someone might see him.
Student read: He worked <u>hungrily</u>, <u>after</u> [omits "that"] someone who might see him.

Text, line 3:   At last he opened the door and <u>stepped</u> inside.
Student read: At last he opened the door and <u>stooped</u> inside.

These errors are much more significant than the ones we saw before. They change the author's meaning. In addition, they change the author's sentences so that they no longer make sense. For example, keys are not skillful, nor can anyone tire them. Yet none of these errors warned this reader that something went wrong, since he did not go back and correct himself. We are dealing with a more serious problem here than faulty word recognition. This youngster is not expecting to make sense out of what he reads. After all, we all make *some* errors in word recognition, but good readers understand that when these errors change the meaning, corrections are indicated. Poor readers don't expect the material to make sense, so that their word-recognition errors don't serve as such signals. They just go on reading.

What Caused These Errors?

Many reading teachers believe that children don't comprehend because they don't recognize (or "decode") the words correctly. I believe the *contrary* is true in many cases—that because children don't expect to comprehend or find sensible, realistic material, they don't correct the decoding errors that violate such expectations. Which of these two situations accurately describes the child you're working with is an important question. The measures you take to correct the problem should depend on what the cause of the problem is.

Fortunately, it's relatively simple to find the real cause. If you've copied the decoding errors of the student as previously suggested, read the material to yourself just as the student read it to you. If his decoding errors violated good sense or normal sentence structure, and these violations did not lead him to go back and make corrections, you know he doesn't expect what he reads to make sense, provided you're seeing his typical reading behavior. But how do you know that his decoding skills are not at fault?

Did he miss words like *and, this,* and *the,* which he has known since first grade? Did he omit or change easy common endings such as *ed, s, es, ing, ly?* Did many or most of his errors occur when he incorrectly decoded easy-to-decode groups of letters that are very common and are pronounced just as you expect them to be pronounced? If he did these things, it's a safe bet that he really knew how to decode those words correctly, and that his real problems are elsewhere. The next chapter will tell you how to deal with his comprehension problems. If you deal with them, you will see that his word recognition (decoding) problems will just about disappear, as if by magic.

Some of you may find it hard to believe that many children who make decoding errors really know the sounds that those letters make. If so, you'll be interested in this incident, which occurred when I tested a fourteen-year-old, normally intelligent boy. He encountered the word *photograph* on a list, and said "pottograph." I asked him to try it again, more carefully. It was still "pottograph." I pointed out that the word began and ended with the same two letters, *p, h,* and that they should be pronounced the same way each time, but he still insisted on "pottograph." I pointed out that he had correctly used the *f* sound for the final *p, h* and asked if that helped. No, it didn't. I asked what sound the letters *p, h* made. He said he didn't know. When I asked again, he insisted he didn't know. Finally,

I said to him, "Are you *sure* you don't know what sound *p, h* makes, Philip?" For eight years Philip had been writing his name, and he'd been hearing it pronounced for fourteen years —and he still said he didn't know what sound its first two letters made. Obviously he did know, but either couldn't or wouldn't use the knowledge.

Earlier in this chapter I mentioned that it is easier to decode words in sentences than it is to decode them when they appear on lists, where the words are not organized in meaningful relationships to each other. In both instances, the reader can use the letters of the word to help him sound it out. But when the word appears in a sentence, the reader has, in addition, the sense of the situation to help him decide what the word is. Kenneth Goodman, a prominent authority in the field of linguistics, goes even further. He says that in contextual situations, good readers don't decode the whole word at all. They decode just as little of it as they possibly can, using their sense of the situation, their knowledge of sentence structure and of word meanings, and of any relevant experience they've had, to help limit their guesses as to the word. Let's do a simple experiment to see if that's true.

What word am I thinking of? I'll give you a hint—it starts with *o.* Now that's pretty silly. You don't have nearly enough information to give you a fighting chance, so it's not very likely that you can guess it.

Suppose I give you the same hint, but put it in a meaningful sentence. "It was very cold out so he put on his o_____." I doubt that you had any trouble in deciding that the word was *overcoat,* even though you couldn't have decoded more than one of its eight letters. Why didn't you guess *oatmeal,* or *over,* or any other word that begins with *o?* Goodman says that your knowledge of sentence structure, word meanings, and experience of reality acted as limiting factors. They helped you to eliminate the words that began with *o* but didn't fit into the meaning of the sentence. If you can get the word right with a minimum of decoding, why do more?

When a youngster decodes unrelated words on a list, he gets

no help from context, and he makes many more errors. Of course, if he recognizes that this is not the normal decoding situation and shifts gears, decoding every part of the word because he has no other useful information, he may be quite accurate in decoding the list of words. The crucial question still is, how well does he decode words in the normal reading situation, where they appear in sensible, meaningful sentences?

I recently studied the decoding errors of one hundred consecutive children who had been referred to the Adelphi University Reading and Learning Disability Center because they apparently had decoding (word-recognition) problems. In decoding a list of words, these children made many errors. I then asked them the following questions about the words they missed. I'd suggest that you use the same questions to learn what you can about your youngster's decoding.

1. "Please look at the word carefully again, and tell me what it is." In response, they got 49.9 percent of the words right that they missed before. Those who answered before or immediately after I finished asking the question rarely got it right. Apparently they hadn't had enough time to look at the word carefully, so they were asked to try it a third time. Often they were then able to get it right. If not, they were then asked the following questions, depending on the situation.

2. If the student omitted a letter (i.e., said "dawn" for *drawn*), I asked: "What are the first two letters?" "What sound do they make?" "What is the word?"

3. If the student distorted a sound (i.e., said "drown" for *drawn*), I asked: "What sound does l-a-w make?" "r-a-w?" "What sound does a-w make?" "So, what is the word?"

Using these questions and other evidence from within the test itself, I concluded that the one hundred children really knew enough to correctly decode more than 90 percent of the words they had missed on their first reading. Please bear in mind that a number of the children I tested were first- and second-graders, and a few others, primarily brain-injured children, had not yet learned to read. Also, this test asked the children to decode a list of words, which is the most difficult way to decode. It is clear to me that the vast majority of junior and high school children know how to decode, even though they make decoding errors.

That really shouldn't surprise any adult. Have you ever added a list of figures when your mind was elsewhere, or when you were very tired, and found yourself saying, "Two and two are five"? Would I be justified in concluding that you didn't know how much two plus two are? Isn't the problem that you really do know, but you just aren't attending to it fully? It would be surprising if the same kind of error didn't also occur in decoding.

On the test I use, many children who try to decode the word *carpenter* whisper to themselves "car, pen, ter"—and then almost shout "chapter!" which they read a few words before this one. Their whispering tells you that they know all the parts of the word. Yet, they haven't held themselves together long enough to use what they know.

Many things can keep a student from paying attention to and using what he knows about decoding. He might be tired. Some other problem might be more important to him at the moment. Or he might be saying to himself: "Reading always makes me uncomfortable. How painful will this be? How 'dumb' will I look? Suppose the person hearing me gets angry? What if I'm not even good enough to satisfy Mom or Dad listening to me?"

But a person has only so much mental energy to give to a task at any one time. If a lot of that is going into worry, or other unproductive (nondecoding) effort, how much is left to think about the reading? Often the person gets so uncomfortable, he has to relieve that pain and stop "grinding" himself against pieces of the problem—so he just guesses. When he does, the answer is almost always wrong. In some ways decoding is even harder than memorizing the addition and subtraction facts. After all, two plus two are always four, but do the letters *o-u*, to cite only one example, always produce the same sound in the words *four, out, through,* and *thorough?* To make matters worse, don't other letter combinations also produce those *o-u* sounds?

In spite of all this, decoding (word recognition) itself is basically a very simple process if you can cut most of the negative feeling out of it. Many children who are retarded, brain-injured, or disturbed (some combine all three) decode successfully, so the process can't be too difficult for the normal child.

Still Need Decoding Help?

If after you determine whether your child knows the decoding facts you still feel he needs some help in decoding, then read the next chapter carefully. If that doesn't seem to fit your student, or for some relatively obscure reason decoding is something he really doesn't know enough about, your best bet is a method called Glass Analysis, or Perceptual Conditioning. Many schools, including our clinic, have used this method for years and taught many children to become successful decoders with it.

There are several things about Glass Analysis that I think lift it head and shoulders above the other decoding techniques.

1. You don't have to teach children abstract rules, or how to use their judgment about decoding words.

2. The method teaches the absolute minimum that you need to know to decode successfully, and not one bit more, so it's efficient.

3. You need no special equipment, books, or expertise to teach it.

4. The student is not likely to have encountered it before, so he won't feel you're pushing him backward to do what he did in the second or third grade.

To understand this method, let's look at what successful decoders do. Try to decode the following word, which you probably haven't seen before—*absquatulate.* Decide how it's pronounced before reading on. The only letters about whose pronunciation there can be any question are the vowels. Chances are that you pronounced the first *a* as in *cab,* the second *a* as in *hot,* the second *u* as in *cute,* and the last *a* as in *fate* or the second *a* in *adequate.* Notice that there were three *a*'s in that word, and that although each was pronounced differently, all of them were correctly pronounced. Why? Did you use phonic rules? (Honestly now, how many phonic rules can you repeat?) Did you break the word up into syllables? (Again, how many of the thirty-odd rules of syllabication can you repeat?) I don't believe we do any of those things when we decode a new word. I think we do the most efficient thing we can. We say to ourselves: "I've seen groups of letters that make up this word in many other words. In those other words the groups had certain typical pronunciations, so I'll use those pronunciations in the new word." And that's the whole secret.

To teach a child how to decode, you have only to teach him which letters to group or cluster together, and how to pronounce each cluster. A cluster is any group of letters that it is useful to learn to decode because it appears in many words. Typical examples would be *est, ark, ph, tion,* and *qu.* We find that children learn to decode properly with this method even though they are said to have so-called visual or auditory discrimination problems, providing they can otherwise see and hear normally. The only other thing they must know is the names of the letters, which will not be a problem for secondary school students. Our experience is that a complete nondecoder has about 125 clusters to learn, and your high school or junior high school student has probably learned most of them by now anyway, so you won't have too many to teach.

Using Glass Analysis

Let's assume that you see the student has trouble decoding a word because he can't correctly pronounce a letter cluster in it, and you decide that you want to teach that letter cluster, because it appears in other words too. Remember we are interested in teaching him the letter cluster, not a specific word. If he learns that cluster, he'll be able to decode many words that have that cluster in it, including the word he missed. Let's assume that the letter cluster you want to teach is *ark*.

Print a few words that contain that letter cluster on separate pieces of paper—*mark, bark, lark, park*. Always show the entire word. Never separate the letter cluster *(ark)* from the rest of the word with your hand or anything else. You want the student to learn to do this in his own head, independently—and he can't do that if you do it for him. And never break up the letters of a cluster in your questioning, as the entire cluster should be learned as a unit.

Present the word and be sure the student continues to look at it as you work with it. Then ask the following questions, in this order.

YOU: "This word is *mark*. What is it?"

STUDENT: "Mark." [If he doesn't know, repeat the entire previous line, first telling him the word and then asking what it is again until he gets it right. It is essential that you stay calm and noncrítical with such errors, or the child will become more agitated and even less capable of attending to the task. A good way for you to calm him down is to stay calm and pleasant yourself. Remember, if a child answers any of these questions incorrectly, and many of them do from time to time, they do so not because these questions are so hard, but because they are anxious and can't pay attention. So, expect the youngster to be anxious, especially the first few times you do this or anything new—and do what you can to lower his level of anxiety.]

YOU: "In the word *mark*, what letter makes the mə sound? [ə is the sound of the letter *o* in *person,* or the *o* in *Marion.*]

STUDENT: "Em." [If the answer is not right, matter-of-factly give the answer yourself, and ask it again, until you get the right answer.]

YOU: "In the word *mark,* what letters make the *ark* sound?"

STUDENT: "Ay, ar, kay." [If this answer or any other answer is not right, see the comment in the previous bracket.]

YOU: "In the word *mark,* what sound does the letter *em* make?"

STUDENT: "m∂."

YOU: "In the word *mark,* what letters make the *ark* sound?"

STUDENT: "Ay, ar, kay."

YOU: "So what is the word?"

STUDENT: "Mark."

Now go on and do *bark, lark,* and *park* in exactly the same way. You will not only be teaching the *ark* cluster, but also the sound of the letters *m, b, l,* and *p* (as parts of the *ark* words).

Once your student masters the *ark* cluster in one-syllable words, use the same technique with the cluster in longer words. Use some words in which the cluster appears in the beginning, others in which it appears in the middle, and others in which it appears at the end of the word.

Now, will the student carry over what you have taught him when he reads other *ark* words? Don't be surprised or disappointed, but the answer is no—unless you gently and supportively teach him to do so. Here's how you do that.

When the student is fairly good at answering your Glass Analysis questions about the *ark* cluster, write several sentences containing these and other *ark* words, and tell your student that you are now going to help him improve his reading by teaching him to use the *ark* cluster when he reads sentences as well as individual words. Ask him to read aloud the sentences you have written. Please observe the following practices. Experience tells us they are very useful.

1. If he has trouble with words that don't contain the *ark* cluster, quickly and pleasantly tell him what the word is. Don't do anything to pull attention away from teaching him how to independently use the *ark* cluster in new words. Do make

a note of the words missed. Later look at them to see if they contain new clusters that you need to teach.

2. If he has trouble decoding either new *ark* words or the ones you've already spent time on, don't be surprised or upset. Ask the following questions:
   a. "Does this word contain any clusters you know?"
   b. "What cluster?"
   c. "What sound does that cluster make?"
   d. "So what is the word?"

In time (and with patience), these questions should become unnecessary. Do not work on any more than two or three clusters in one lesson—less if that many seem to be confusing.

Does Glass Analysis work? The Adelphi University Reading and Learning Disability Center did a carefully controlled experiment with it in an elementary school in New York City. This school had about half its children bused in from ghetto areas. Many of those children were from broken homes and welfare families.

As it worked out, those were the children we worked with exclusively. That school had five classes in each grade, and the classes were grouped strictly by ability. When we explained our experiment, the teachers of the average or better classes said: "Our children are doing fine in decoding, so why bother to try a new method that may not work?" That left us with the bottom two classes of grades one to five. In those classes poor attendance, discipline problems, and learning difficulties were common. Dr. Glass (who developed this technique) and I felt that if Glass Analysis worked with these children, it had to be good.

I tested the ability of each of these 350 children to decode, once before we taught them this technique, and once afterward. Between times, paraprofessionals worked with five or six children at a time, a few times a week. Now remember that, like you, these people were not trained teachers. If they can give this help, you can too. At the end of a year, these "poor academic risk" children gained an average of slightly over three years in decoding. I'm convinced that this is the best method of teaching decoding that has yet been developed.

There are commercially prepared materials for Glass Analysis. You can get price lists and other information by writing to Easier-to-Learn, P. O. Box 329, Garden City, N. Y. 11530. However, using the suggestions I've made, you can prepare your own materials.

Suppose your child misses words in which the letters are not sounded just as expected—words like *tongue, laugh,* and so on. It doesn't pay to teach them the *ue* in *tongue* is silent, or that the *augh* in laugh is pronounced *aff,* because those clusters just don't appear in enough other words to make it worthwhile. The only thing you can do with these relatively rare clusters (which don't have the sounds usually associated with those letters) is to say: "That word is tongue" (or whatever it is) when it is not read correctly. More important, if these are common words and your student still misses them, it's a good bet that your student hasn't done much reading on his own. Otherwise, he would have encountered these common words enough times to have learned how to say them correctly. How to encourage your child to read on his own is something I'll discuss in a later chapter.

In any case, now that you've explored your youngster's decoding, tell him what you've found, in a positive way. Most likely you will have learned that there is no real decoding problem, and that you can forget your concerns about it. Your behavior should show that you can calmly accept the errors that you (and maybe he) previously thought were signs of trouble. In fact, we've seen that some of them are actually signs of strength. Many youngsters will be relieved to learn that their apparent errors are not really a cause for concern.

A small minority of older youngsters do have a decoding problem. That is, they consistently don't know what sounds to associate with the printed symbols. If your youngster is one of these, it's doubly important that you react calmly to his errors, because if he gets agitated, it will be much harder for him to

decode correctly. Use Glass Analysis with such a youngster—
not just one or two lessons, but as many as ten or twelve may
be necessary to see if he can be helped. If your youngster
doesn't start to "catch on," read Appendix E of this book to see
where to go from here.

CHAPTER 4

"It's boring!" Or, "Why do I need to know about (sniff) that?"

Sometimes our students complain about their school-work. They tell us that the work isn't interesting, or that they have no real need to learn that particular topic—usually one they don't like. When some parents and teachers hear those comments, they take them at face value and think that they describe the real problem. They try to make the work more interesting, if they can. If they can't, they may abandon the topic altogether and use "games," or else try to tie the subject into some other area the student is interested in, like sports.

This approach appears to work. The child is more comfortable and, often for the first time, willingly goes along with the assignment.

But fundamental questions remain: Do the children learn the skills they need in such activities? Do they then use those skills when they read their textbooks in social studies, math, or other areas? I suspect that the answer, especially to the clearly crucial second question, is no. Many youngsters see these activities as respites, as substitutes for academic work. In other words, they don't see these activities as more pleasant ways to learn schoolwork. They see them as ways to avoid it.

When children say that reading is boring, or that they don't like it, I think that's like saying that there is no kind of food that they like. After all, you need both food and reading to be a healthy, well-developed person. Further, food comes in infinite varieties of textures, temperatures, and flavors. I doubt that anyone can truthfully say that he doesn't like any food. Reading material also comes in an infinite variety. It deals with every topic, at every level of difficulty, at any length, and in every mood from the most humorous to the most tragic. How can anyone say that they don't like any kind of reading? I suspect that for these people, the problem is not within reading, but within them.

Does Everything Have to Be Interesting?

The idea of making work more interesting just because a weak student says it's boring is often wrong, in and of itself. The truth is that some things we learn *are* boring, and there is no way to get around that. Did you learn the multiplication tables because they were interesting? Are you better off for having learned them? Does the Internal Revenue Service care if filling out your income tax form is an interesting task? Boring or not, your own self-interest demands that you get it done in time, and as carefully as you can. I don't think we do the youngsters a favor when we say to them: "If you don't find that interesting, you don't have to do it."

The Real Problem Is Something Else

More important, if you told your doctor that you had a painful sore throat, you would expect him to do more than just relieve the symptom. The symptom bothers the patient because of the pain. It bothers the doctor for other reasons. He knows that the pain is caused by an infection. So the doctor sees the symptom as an indication of something more serious. He tests to see what specific germ or virus is causing it, and then prescribes medicine that will knock it out.

However, when children say that reading or schoolwork bores them, many of us assume that the youngster is reading competently and is bored with it. We try to change the activity to something more interesting. In other words we deal with the symptom, not the cause.

Many other pupils say that they can read all right, but they can't remember what they read. It's no coincidence that this comment and the one that reading is boring are almost always made by people who have trouble understanding what they read. In my experience both comments come from the same problem, which is a common and pervasive one that most of us overlook because we find it hard to believe that anyone could have difficulty with such a simple-looking process. These people usually have enormous problems with literal comprehension.

Literal Comprehension

What is literal comprehension? It's the ability to pay attention to and recall directly stated information that is easy to understand. Let me illustrate. Here is a short passage.

> General Smith thought he could defend the port against the British with two battalions of men. However, when he got there, he asked General Jones for three more battalions.

Here are some literal comprehension questions on the above passage. Below each one is an answer that might be given by an otherwise normal child who has difficulty with literal comprehension. Although all of the answers that follow each question are typical and wrong, it's a rare child who would get all three wrong.

How many battalions did he think he'd need at first?
Three.

Who asked for more troops?
Jones.

What was General Smith defending?
His troops.

Please note that I'm *not* talking about questions like:

How many battalions did General Smith want altogether?

Was defending the port easier or harder than Smith first thought it would be?

These are not literal comprehension questions, since they ask for information that is not directly stated in the passage.

"Now wait a minute," you may say. "My youngster isn't doing well in school, but he certainly knows what simple, directly stated material tells him." Well, the plain truth of the matter is that a great many youngsters do not know, including some who don't say they're bored by school and reading. But whether they voice it or not, that boredom makes perfect sense to me. How can they become interested in material when they don't know what it says? In any case, don't assume anything. A little later I will show you how you can easily find out if your youngster has this problem. If you find out that he doesn't, you needn't bother with the rest of this chapter. But if he has the problem and doesn't understand what it says when the reading is easy, how can we expect him to draw conclusions from it or to understand it when it's difficult?

Here is a typical example from my own teaching experience.

A youngster read a passage about volcanoes. The passage repeatedly and clearly stated that these volcanoes were in Hawaii, and then said: "Of course, the volcanoes in this area are no longer active." I told the youngster to read the sentence and ask himself if he understood it. He was told to ask me about anything in it that he didn't understand, and when he finished, I was going to ask him questions about it. After my questions, he was free to look back at the text. He read the sentence aloud correctly, and insisted immediately that he understood it and needed no explanations. I asked: "What does the word *active* mean, as used in this sentence?" Without looking back at the text, he quickly wrote the answer: "Running, jumping around." I substituted his definition in the text and said, "Then the sentence means that these volcanoes are no longer running and jumping around. Is that right?" Embarrassed, he admitted his definition was wrong. I suggested that we start over. He should reread the sentence and ask me to clarify any parts of it that he did not understand. As before, he read it quickly and assured me that he understood it. I suspect that he only looked to see if it had any unfamiliar words. Finding none, he felt it offered no comprehension problem. My next question was: "What do the words *in this area* mean, as used in this sentence?" Again, without referring to the text, he quickly wrote: "In New York City." Then he looked at his answer and struck his forehead with his palm. He lived in New York City, and he knew there were no volcanoes there. So he crossed out his last answer and wrote, "In upstate New York." Did this boy understand simple, directly stated information? Did he know that he didn't understand it? Of course what he reads is boring. If it doesn't have meaning, how can it be interesting?

When these youngsters can't tell what easy material means, we get very upset. We can't understand how anyone could think that volcanoes run or jump around, or could possibly be in New York when the article says many times over that they are in Hawaii. It is frightening to feel that their way of comprehending is miles away from ours, and is incomprehensible to us.

Poor comprehension of easy material generally comes from two causes. Let's talk about the more common one first. In the first case, the youngster knows that theoretically, reading is supposed to make sense—but that knowledge remains theoretical. He doesn't apply it, and so he doesn't dig for the meaning when he reads. He thinks that good reading means sounding out the words well, and reading with good pace and expression —but no more. Sometimes when I ask one of these youngsters an easy question about something he's just read, he's surprised. He says, "If you had told me I had to know what it said, I would have paid attention to that too." So I warn him that that's what I want, and we do another paragraph. It rarely helps—he doesn't do any better, even with the warning, because he's just not used to reading that way.

Other kids are so worried about decoding that they don't have any effort left over to devote to getting the meanings. Still other kids know they're supposed to pay attention to the meaning, but a lot of their mental energy goes into other things. As they read they worry about how uncomfortable they'll be if they don't "get it." Will we be angry with them? Will they feel stupid? There's too little energy left to think about the meaning, so they "lose" some or all of it.

Changing this may take a few months, but it isn't too hard. The technique I recommend was designed by Anthony Manzo, a professor of education at the University of Missouri at Kansas City. Work with nonfiction that isn't too difficult. Use a chapter your student's history teacher has assigned him to read, if you can. That way your work benefits the student immediately, and he can see that the technique has practical value. Introduce the lesson by telling him that this work will help him with his comprehension. Have him read at least a short paragraph in his textbook, then turn the book over. Now he (or you, if need be) should write down every one of that paragraph's ideas that he can remember. They won't be organized in any special way. Don't worry if they are inaccurate or incomplete—just continue writing them down until he can't think of any more.

Now we check up on what was written. Were the ideas remembered accurately? Open the text and make whatever corrections are needed. Next, were all the important ideas remembered? Again, check the text, and add the missing ideas. Now we have a full group of correct ideas, but they aren't organized, so that's our next job.

Take another sheet of paper. If you think your youngster can do it, ask him to suggest a good title for what he has read. If he can't, use the heading in the text, or provide one yourself. (Make sure you've studied the text in advance, so that you have a good descriptive title.) Write that down at the top of the new piece of paper. Now if he has read more than a paragraph, ask him for the first important (or main) idea. Again, provide it if he is unable to do so (either quoting the text or producing it yourself). Then, using outline form, copy all the ideas from the first list that belong under the main idea. Use the same procedure for the other main ideas and details. If you start with one paragraph at a time, the job is somewhat shorter and easier. Move your pupil to two paragraphs or more, as soon as he does well with one. Always start at the beginning of a topic, however. Try to finish at a logical stopping point in the text too— or at least pick it up at the same spot so you can finish it next time.

Another group of children has a different problem in literal comprehension. Unlike the group we just talked about, these children don't pay attention to meaning because they don't expect what they read to make sense.

To help these children understand better, we cannot hope to superimpose our way of comprehending on them. First we need to understand how they comprehend, and then help *them to change from where they are.* They can't change themselves from where we are. I'll explain how these poor literal comprehenders think about their reading.

How Good Literal Comprehenders Correct Their Errors

First, let's talk about how good literal comprehenders operate, in order to see more clearly what poor comprehenders do that is different. Let's assume that we are reading late at night. Suddenly we realize that we don't have the slightest idea of the contents of the last two or three pages. So we either stop and reread or decide to put the book away and reread the last few pages when we can pay more attention to them.

Or, we are reading the *New York Times* and it says that New York City's welfare bill for the coming year will be $37.46. Again, we stop and reread, because we are sure that this figure is not correct.

Assume that we are reading the newspaper again, and find the following.

The injured driver
State Police responded by
for himself and the others.

We reach the end of the first line and expect the sentence to continue on the next one. However, there is no connection between the second line and the other two. So we quickly search the rest of the column to try to locate the missing line. We stop reading to see where the error is.

These three incidents have striking, important common elements.

1. In each case, something within us, as competent readers, told us to stop and try to figure out what was wrong. Neither the text nor anyone sitting next to us had to tell us to stop? Why?

2. Apparently we came to the printed material expecting that it would have certain characteristics. In the reading-late-at-night incident, we obviously expected to be communicated with when we read. In the welfare incident we expected the news story to be consistent with what we know the cost of welfare to be. In the missing-line incident we stopped because we expect sentences to make sense.

3. When the information coming from the printed page violated our expectation for it, we stopped. In fact, we use this violation as a warning signal—it tells us that we have not grasped the ideas presented by the author, and will have to stop and work harder to grasp them.

Without such an internal warning system, we would never know if we were getting the ideas that the author wanted us to, and that would be a disaster. We pass our knowledge on to others through print. Would you ride on a bridge or in a car designed by someone who couldn't tell if he understood what the author of his textbook on safety in designing meant? Civilization couldn't continue if we had no way of knowing whether or not we understood correctly the discoveries of the previous generations.

How Some Poor Literal Comprehenders Function

Do people who are not competent literal comprehenders read in the same way? Here are two incidents, out of many in my own teaching, that cast light on the question. Henry, a thirteen-year-old, mistakenly read to me: "The knight mounted his horse and rode into the bottle." The last word should have been *battle,* of course. But he went right on reading, unaware of the error. When I asked him questions designed to get him to think about whether or not what he just said could be true, he impatiently said: "What do you want from me? I read it, didn't I?"

Albert, a fourteen-year-old, had failed a third-grade literal comprehension task. That is, although the material was easy to understand, he could not tell me enough about what it said to pass at that grade level. I asked him to read it aloud. Two of the printed sentences said:

The boys were afraid. They thought it was a bear.

He read them as:

The boys were after they thought it was a bear.

In other words, he said "after" instead of "afraid," and read the whole thing as though it were one sentence instead of two. When I read his version of it to him, he seemed to be quite content with it, so I then asked him if it made sense. His reply was: "It doesn't have to make sense. They often put stuff like that in just to see if you're awake."

Neither Henry nor Albert expected to make sense out of what they read. In fact, Albert had developed a rationale that explained to him why printed material *didn't* make sense. Neither of the boys could compare the ideas he got from the text to a set of expectations that told him whether or not he had gotten the author's ideas correctly. Therefore they, unlike the competent literal comprehender, did not get a signal to stop and go back when they had made an error.

The fundamental difference between competent and these noncompetent literal comprehenders is not that one has more skill in answering comprehension questions than the other. That's only a by-product. The competent comprehender reads the material differently in the first place. He understands it correctly because he demands that it make sense, be internally consistent, and match reality if it is nonfiction or realistic fiction. When you ask him a comprehension question, he produces an answer that is consistent with reality and the author's ideas. The reason his answer is correct is that he draws it from information he reads correctly.

But the noncompetent literal comprehender presents a completely different picture. He reads the text passively. He lacks a useful set of expectations for it. He is content to read parts of it that have no meaning to him at all. The ideas he grasps need not be consistent with each other or with reality. And he has no way to determine if his understanding of the text is consistent with the author's. When we ask him a literal comprehension question, he produces an answer from his partly incorrect view of the material. Worse yet, he has no way of knowing from within himself whether or not that answer is correct. What makes an answer right? Obviously, if the teacher likes it, for her own obscure and mysterious reasons, it's right. For such a youngster this is a frightening game without rules. It offers him no way to improve himself.

How do we know that these youngsters can't tell for themselves if their answers are right or wrong? Listen to the way their voices rise as they give an answer. They say: "The answer is fourteen?" questioning whether or not their answer is right. Then their eyes continue to search the teacher's face until her decision is evident. Would they react this way if they knew the answer was right from within themselves?

Lastly, when these children give a wrong answer and the teacher tells them to try again, they usually give one inappropriate response after another. Finally, by elimination, they hit upon the right one. Would they give even the first answer if they knew beforehand that it was wrong? Having learned that it was wrong, doesn't the fact that they give other inappropriate responses (while watching the teacher's face) tell us that they still don't know what the characteristics of a correct answer are? In fact, if we don't do something to show them how they independently can tell if they are reading and answering questions correctly, then we must either stand by their elbows to tell them that for the rest of their lives or admit that we have failed, and that they never will become independent readers.

Who Are These Poor Literal Comprehenders?

How can we recognize the children who don't have or use the proper expectations for written material? Here is a list of some of their most obvious symptoms. Where necessary, I have told why the symptom appears.

Symptom 1. These children make decoding errors (don't say the printed words correctly). When these errors change the author's meaning, they are not aware of it and make no effort to correct it. (Now you know why I suggested in the previous chapter on decoding that it might be important to read this chapter. These children can almost always decode the word correctly if they look at it again. However, that's the rub. They don't expect the sentence to make sense. There is no feedback to tell them that an error has been made that needs correcting. When I did remedial work with high school children I kept track of how many decoding errors they made, but did no work with them on decoding. Instead, I used a technique called "Structured Comprehension," which I will describe shortly, to teach them what characteristics printed material has, so they could judge for themselves whether or not they understood it correctly. Their decoding errors all but disappeared as they learned to do this, in spite of the fact that I made no attempt to teach them anything about decoding.)

Symptom 2. If you ask them to tell you what or who the pronouns (*he, she, it,* etc.) in a given sentence stand for, they are usually wrong. (This is because they do not realize that each printed sentence makes sense, and is connected in meaning to the sentence before and after it. They are passive and don't try to establish those connections.)

Symptom 3. A common word often has several meanings. These youngsters can't tell us which meaning applies when the word is used in a sentence. In the examples below, multi-meaning words are underlined. Can your student correctly define those words as used here? (If not, he doesn't understand that he must select the meaning of the word that is consistent with the rest of the sentence, because sentences must make sense.)

a. I've lost that <u>spring</u>, and this engine won't <u>run</u> without it.

b. I just can't <u>see</u> playing a joke on him. After all, he came <u>expressly</u> to see how you were.

c. He was a tall man, and a <u>lean</u> <u>one</u>.

In some cases more than one meaning is acceptable, so I'm including the definitions.

a. spring — a piece of metal designed to return to its original shape after it's bent

run — operate, work properly

b. see — understand, agree to

expressly — specifically and only

c. lean — thin, slim

one — man (as used here)

Symptom 4. For the same reason, the youngster does not use the dictionary voluntarily because it only confuses him. (Suppose he finds a word he doesn't understand in a sentence, and looks it up. If the dictionary gives several definitions for the word, he doesn't know which one to take. He doesn't understand that he should pick the definition that makes the sentence sensible and consistent with the sentences around it.

To see if this is a problem, have him use the dictionary to find the meanings of the underlined words in the examples given under Symptom 3.)

Symptom 5. He doesn't know the meaning of figurative expressions such as "Fred was in a fog," or "He swung a haymaker at his opponent." Common proverbs such as "You can't tell a book by its cover" are not understood. This youngster feels that "tell" means to talk to and "by" means near. He wonders why anyone would tell anything to a book. If they did for some reason, of course they'd do it near its cover. (Albert would say: "This is just another proof that reading isn't supposed to make sense." Frequently the student feels he never heard that proverb before. Why not? How can we remember what we didn't understand in the first place?)

To test for this symptom, tell a story about a poor boy who desperately wants a bike. He slowly and painstakingly saves up enough money to buy one. Then when he has the money and is only waiting for the store to open so that he can finally have it, a member of his family becomes ill. He contributes or lends the money toward the medical expenses. Then say simply, "Don't count your chickens before they hatch." Now ask the youngster if he can tell you what that sentence means, and why it is the final sentence of the story.

Symptom 6. With the text in front of him, he will be unable to tell you as accurately as he should what it was he just read, in easy-to-grasp material, when you ask him questions. Your questions should not ask him to change information given in the text, which would be far more difficult, but only to repeat it. If he is a poor literal comprehender, he's also unlikely to refer to the text to find the correct answer.

Symptom 7. Authors frequently leave small gaps in meaning. This makes for greater brevity. They assume that the reader will actively try to fill in the missing information. Here are some examples of what I mean and some questions to see if your student is trying to fill in the gaps to get the meaning.

a. Dollars to doughnuts that my horse can run faster than yours. (What does "Dollars to doughnuts" mean, and what is its connection to the rest of this sentence?)

b. After the dough is mixed it is put into holding vats. In a few hours it rises to twice its original size. (Why is the dough put into holding vats?)

c. When it got dark, Washington's army marched out quietly. Only a few men were left behind, with orders to keep the campfires going all night. (Why didn't the army leave during the daylight hours?)

Symptom 8. These students are very poor at understanding difficult passages. Whether the passage is easy or difficult, they cannot successfully use their own judgment to grasp the author's purpose or most important idea, draw conclusions, or in any way use the text to help produce new ideas or understandings not stated by the author. If these students are not sufficiently aware of what easy, directly stated material tells them, how can they understand material that is difficult? How can they adequately use any of the higher level comprehension skills when all those skills assume success with something they cannot do—understand the author's direct statements, just for starters?

Although the eight symptoms listed appear to involve separate reading skills, they often flow from the same cause—the inability to find and use appropriate expectations to which students can compare the ideas reading offers them. This they must do to see if they really are "tuning in" to what the author said. Working on these eight characteristics as though they themselves were sources of difficulty, rather than symptoms of that deeper problem, usually fails.

The technique I developed to overcome the problem I call Structured Comprehension.

Doing Structured Comprehension

Structured Comprehension is something the tutor must practice to learn to do it effectively. In addition, the student using it improves only gradually. After all, he has spent many years getting to be the way he is, and can't be expected to change in a few weeks or months. In fact, the older student may take one to two years to straighten out his literal comprehension problem completely. Don't be discouraged—he will be showing improvement during most of that time, even though it is common to see a little backsliding now and then.

Maybe you don't have the time to practice to learn to use this technique, or the ability to accept the youngster's difficulties when you see how pervasive they are. In that case turn the problem and everything you have learned about it over to someone else—a reading clinic, or a tutor. Possibly you and a neighbor can work out an arrangement in which you tutor his child while he tutors yours. Both youngsters and their parents may be able to get at the problem more calmly that way.

In any case, expect to make mistakes as you learn this technique, and don't be upset when you do. The only people I know who don't make mistakes are the people in cemeteries. It's rare that making a mistake permanently or seriously damages a relationship, particularly when we recognize that the other person's intentions were good.

Selecting material of appropriate difficulty is important. If the reading is too easy for him, the student won't see the necessity of changing his way of approaching the material. If it is too difficult, you will have to spend too much time explaining the background of the material and won't be able to spend enough time on the lesson itself. I usually find that the student's social studies book is a good compromise between these two extremes, and better for this purpose than his math and science books.

Provide the student with a notebook of at least fifty pages and a pen. For now, it is your job, not the student's, to see to it that these two items, plus a good dictionary and the text you will use, appear at every lesson. It is your job because the children who need this help are disorganized and poorly motivated. You can avoid a great deal of unnecessary and counterproductive friction if you don't give your youngster an opportunity to forget to bring these materials, to be "wrong" again. Besides, if you plan a lesson that demands the use of these materials and at the last moment they are not there, you will have nothing to teach, and may become quite frustrated and angry.

Now read the first line of the textbook passage aloud while the student reads it silently. I always do this in the first few lessons, to relieve the student of the anxiety of reading the words aloud incorrectly. You and the student are going to concentrate on comprehension and don't want to get sidetracked by decoding or anything else. Don't feel that the passage is too difficult if in subsequent lessons when the student reads it himself, he makes many decoding errors (doesn't say the words correctly). As explained before, in older children these errors are rarely due to lack of decoding skill. They occur because the student doesn't expect the text's ideas to make sense, so he doesn't feel the need to be accurate with the words that convey the ideas. Decoding errors disappear automatically and gradually, as the student learns that the ideas he reads must make sense.

After the sentence is read, I tell the student that he should ask himself if he understands the sentence—all of it. If he does not understand it, he can ask me as many questions about it as he needs to, and I answer them. The student should be told that once he finishes asking his questions, you are going to ask your questions. He will write his answers as briefly as possible in the notebook you have provided. Make it clear that after you ask your questions he is welcome to look back at the textbook to find the answers.

Don't be surprised if he fails to ask any questions or look back at the book during the first few lessons. Students rarely do at first—so don't be annoyed or disappointed.

It's important to answer the student's questions in a way that shows respect for him. For one thing, if you don't respect your student you shouldn't be working with him. Students who feel that others do not respect them are less likely to respect themselves. They are therefore less likely to expose themselves by showing others the results of their judgment. As a consequence, they often guess impulsively rather than try to figure out answers.

There is another reason for respecting the student who asks questions, no matter how simple they appear to be. But first, congratulate yourself. You have encouraged this student, maybe for the first time, to drop his passivity and ask, "Do I really understand what this says? If not, what can I do to improve my understanding?" That's real progress. If you show a lack of respect for this student's forward step, he is less likely to try to make another. Remember, you are working with him because he has a problem, not because he is good at comprehension. His questions may appear to you to require such self-evident, easy answers that you will be tempted to get despondent or angry. Don't do either. If you are wise you will think about the student's questions. They tell you where he needs help in comprehension. If you use this information in this and subsequent lessons, he will make even more progress. Always look to see what the student's work tells you about both his difficulties and his strengths.

Occasionally we find a youngster who begins to ask many questions. At first we are very happy to have this happen, but soon the questions disturb us. Many of them ask for such simple, obvious information that we think that the pupil really knows the answers and is merely asking a lot of questions in order to keep the instructor from asking his. But I have found that only a few pupils do this. Most of these children are so unsure of themselves and dependent that they are comfortable only if they double-check what they think they know. The necessity to double-check comes from the feeling that in general, or at least in doing schoolwork, they are not competent. Therefore, they find it difficult to trust their own judgment and must confirm what they know by asking us about it. As a tutor you want to encourage people to ask about the things they really do not know. You also want the dependent youngster to have a bit more faith in himself. If you show annoyance at the youngster for asking about simple, obvious things, you are doing two things you really do not want to do. You are corroborating the youngster's judgment that he really is not competent (which makes it more difficult for him to apply himself to solve his comprehension problems). You also make it more difficult for him to feel comfortable in asking his own comprehension questions. If you observe that this youngster is dependent in other areas, then probably his questions are motivated by dependency rather than the need to manipulate. If I feel that's the case, the next time that youngster asks me a question I feel he probably knows the answer to, I say to him: "I have faith that you are smart enough to know the answer to that question. Tell me what you think the answer is. If the answer isn't right, or if you don't know, I'll tell you, but tell me what you think it is first." I don't take the child to task for asking. I indicate that I have faith in his ability to answer it unassisted. After I have used this response a few times, many dependent children no longer ask for the answers to obvious questions, but are still comfortable enough to ask for the answers to more difficult questions.

Again, don't expect your student to ask you any questions in the first few Structured Comprehension lessons. In my experience, he rarely does—because he is unaware that he doesn't know what the material says. It's up to you to awaken him to that truth, as gently and pleasantly as possible.

Here is a sample exercise. The two-sentence statement is from a social studies textbook.

SAMPLE STRUCTURED COMPREHENSION EXERCISE

(Always introduce the topic briefly.)

The pupil should learn that the new material does not stand

alone. Its meaning can only be seen when he understands how it fits into a larger body of connected thought.

Sentence 1: The size of her population is a problem to Japan.

Sentence 2: Today, with her position in the world greatly expanded, this problem is even more frightening in size and complexity.

After you read the first sentence to the student, he should ask as many questions as he needs to, in order to be sure that he understands the whole sentence. Then, writing as briefly as possible on the first empty page of his notebook, he answers the following questions, looking back at the text if he chooses.

QUESTIONS TO BE ANSWERED AFTER READING SENTENCE 1

1. The word *her* as used in sentence 1 tells us that someone has something. Who has something according to that sentence?

2. What is Japan said to have?

3. What does the word *population* mean as used in sentence 1?

4. When sentence 1 says "the size of her population," it means:
   a. How tall Japan's people are.
   b. How heavy Japan's people are.
   c. How many people Japan has.

(In answering this and all other multiple-choice questions, the pupil writes the number of the question, followed by the letter a, b, or c.)

5. Sentence 1 means:
   a. How Japan's people worry about Japan.
   b. Japan worries about how tall her people are becoming.
   c. Japan worries about the large number of people she has.

Now, read sentence 2 to the student. As before, let him ask as many questions as necessary to be sure he understands the sentence. Then he should write down the answers to the following questions.

QUESTIONS TO BE ANSWERED AFTER READING SENTENCE 2:

6. The word *Today* as used in sentence 2 means:

   a. March 18 (or whatever date it is actually), but not other days.

   b. March 18, and two weeks before and after that date.

   c. For the past several years, now, and probably for the next several years.

7. The word *her* as used in sentence 2 means whose? (This is not a multiple-choice question).

8. The words *position in the world* as used in sentence 2 mean:

   a. Placement on the map.

   b. Her place as a powerful, respected nation.

   c. Placement on the globe.

9. The words *greatly expanded* as used in sentence 2 mean:

   a. Much larger.

   b. A little larger.

   c. About the same size as they were before.

10. What do the words *this problem* stand for, as used in sentence 2?

   a. The large number of people who live in Japan.

   b. Japan itself.

   c. The world.

11. What does the word *complexity* mean as used in sentence 2?

   a. Like a duplex, or double.

   b. The large number of smaller parts or problems within the big problem.

   c. Neither a nor b.

12. Sentence 2 means that the Japanese are

   a. More worried.

   b. Less worried.

   c. Just about as worried now about their population problem as they were when they were a less important nation in the world.

13. Where should we look to find out what problems Japan is having because she has so many people?

   a. In sentence 1.

   b. In sentence 2.

   c. The sentences after sentence 2.

Now let's see what these questions try to do, and how they do it.

You may have been surprised that I asked thirteen questions about only two sentences. At this rate, it would take months to cover a whole chapter. But in teaching people how to comprehend, it's necessary for them to learn that every single part of every sentence was put there for the purpose of giving them information, and that absolutely none of it can be disregarded without running the risk of leaving out something important. This is one of the internalized expectations we want these youngsters to have each time they read something. So every single piece of the sentence must be clearly understood, and you as a tutor must know which parts of the sentence need explaining. How will you know if you don't ask? If you are in doubt and think that a question is too easy, ask it anyway. The worst that can happen is that the student will feel good because he got it right. If he doesn't get it right, you have an excellent opportunity to explain a word, a phrase, or principle that your student will need to know in this and in many other sentences.

To make sure each part of each sentence is understood, here are the kinds of information to ask for:

1. The meaning of every common, multi-meaning word and of every unusual word—as they apply in that sentence.

2. The meaning of every figurative expression—as it applies in that sentence. (Figurative expressions, such as "It's raining cats and dogs," have a meaning other than the one their words directly state.)

3. The implied (unstated) connections between the author's ideas. These are very common. See the examples earlier in this chapter.

4. The meaning of every proverb, and how it applies to the situation described in the text.

5. The person or thing that each pronoun (*he, she, who, their, it, them,* etc.) stands for. The correct answer may vary from sentence to sentence, even if you are asking about the same pronouns.

6. The meaning of every word or phrase that is not immediately apparent. I have never yet met a student who needed Structured Comprehension who knew what the words *the former* and *the latter* meant. Nor have I ever met one who understood that when we say "The fox is a sly animal!" we are not talking about just one fox, but really mean practically all foxes.

7. The combined meaning of all implicit and explicit sentence parts. Once each of those parts is understood, we need to make sure that all of them are integrated into the same thought as the author intended. There is a big difference between John who says: "That's a piece of string, two connected metal pieces, and some beads," and Fred who looks at the same objects and says: "That's a necklace." Fred sees the objects in relationship to one another and understands the purpose of that relationship, while John does not. If you go back to the sample Structured Comprehension exercise cited earlier in this chapter, you will see that for the first sentence, questions 1 through 4 help the reader to clarify each detail, but question 5 asks the reader to integrate or connect each of those pieces in the same way as the author did. For the second sentence, after questions 6 through 11 explain the details, question 12 demands their integration.

8. In order to clarify the meaning of the sentence, you should where necessary direct your student to go to the sentence before or after. My question 13 helps to make pupils aware

that the topic discussed in one sentence will continue to be discussed as the passage goes on. Many of my pupils have told me that they thought that each sentence in a paragraph dealt with a different topic.

Following your questions, ask the student to make a simple drawing of the situation described in the sentence or, to save time, prepare three simple drawings in advance and ask your student to choose the one that most accurately represents the situation. It is important to get him in the habit of visualizing what the text says whenever you can.

Questions to Avoid

When you make up Structured Comprehension questions, you may be tempted to ask questions that do not really test the youngster's understanding. Even professional teachers do this sometimes. In the sentence below, I have intentionally used nonsense words.

The garmus began to thrink a full fradget.

1. What began to thrink the fradget?
2. What did the garmus thrink?

If a thousand people answered these questions after reading the sentence, most of them would score 100 percent. However, not a single one of them would understand what the sentence meant. Correctly answering questions without understanding meaning is particularly easy to do when the language of the question follows the language of the text. To get the answer, just follow the language of both the question and the text until the text fills in the gap that the question leaves. Even if your question is more sophisticated—"What is the relationship between the garmus and the fradget?"—you can get credit by saying that the garmus thrinks the fradget, without having any idea of the meaning of "thrinks."

To determine whether the reader actually knows what the sentence means, you must ask him to define each of the troublesome words or phrases (as used in this particular sentence), and then ask him a question that will require him to integrate all of these definitions into the author's connected thought. If I arbitrarily assign the following definitions to the nonsense words, I can then make up an integrative question.

garmus — door of a mining shaft

thrink — open and send out

fradget — a car used to carry miners to and from the mine.

Integration question: The text suggests that the miners' work-day is:

    a. About to start.

    b. About to end.

    c. Can't tell.

Tell why you chose your answer.

Of course, the correct answer is b., since "thrink" theoretically means to open and send out. Since the miners are coming out of the mine, their workday is probably over.

Above all, don't ask "cutesy" (inappropriate) questions. I define those as:

1. Questions the student does not need to answer to understand what the passage says. (For example—What kind of engine supplies the power for the fradget?)

2. Questions that call for more advanced skills than literal comprehension. (For example—What is the main idea of this passage?) Remember, you are using Structured Comprehension because this student can't grasp the relatively easy, directly stated information in single sentences. The more advanced skills can come only after this lower level skill ceases to be a problem.

3. Questions that the student cannot find the answer to in the text, unless the student must know this information to allow literal comprehension of the passage. (For example, if the author uses a term without defining it, the reader must find out what the word means, or risk losing comprehension.)

You should ask a question about every single point that might be a hole in the literal comprehension of the student. You should never ask less, and there is no need to ask for any more, for now.

The average Structured Comprehension lesson takes about forty-five minutes. During that time ask the pupil about ten questions. If you need to, ask a few more so that you don't leave a sentence until its meaning is clear and complete. Otherwise you will reinforce the pupil's basic problem—his belief that sentences don't have to be meaningful, which is the very idea you are trying to eliminate through Structured Comprehension.

Dealing with Answers

As the tutor asks each question, the student writes his answer down in his notebook. Answers are to be written as briefly and clearly as possible, but they must be written. Spoken answers disappear into the air. It's easy for a student to delude himself about how correct they were. I want the student to see clear proof that he must change the way he comprehends now. I also use the written assignments to prove to him that he is making progress. How I do that is described later in the chapter.

However, although all the answers are written, I always tell my students that there is no need to write in complete sentences. Because I want them to concentrate on grasping the literal meaning of the passage, I don't demand (for quite some time) that their spelling or punctuation be correct. The pace of these lessons is important too and should not be permitted to drag. For that reason you should discuss and mark the answer to each question immediately after it is written.

You also don't want the student to find out that he has done all or most of the comprehension questions wrong when it's too late to do anything about it. If he sees that he gets some or all of the first few questions wrong in a situation in which he himself is still respected and, at the same time, is being offered a way to do it better, he will try harder and get more right.

Building Useful Expectations

You may remember that I was quite critical about teaching methods that do not help the student to judge if the answer he is about to write is correct. This problem occurs because the pupil does not bring (or use) a set of useful expectations about the nature of the text to his reading. I pointed out that competent literal comprehenders compare the ideas they get from the text to these expectations. They are thus able to know if they are getting the ideas that the author wanted to convey. It is from these correct ideas in turn that they produce their correct answers to the teacher's questions.

How can we help the poor literal comprehender to learn and apply a useful set of expectations to what he reads? This extremely important part of the lesson comes with the discussion that follows after each answer is written. Don't tell the student if the answer is right or wrong. Instead, ask the student: "How can we tell if your answer is right?" Wait to hear what the student says. If the student really needs this work, he will be unable to judge the aptness of the answer. I then tell my student: "I know how to tell if it's right or wrong. If you learn my trick, you'll be able to tell too. Then you'll get a lot more answers right, because you'll know which ones are wrong *before* you write them down, and you will be able to change them and make them right." At this point, all you have to do is clearly and pleasantly make explicit which specific expectation you have for this material that the student's answer violated. I know that doesn't sound clear or easy, so here is an example.

Text says: Because he didn't know how to use the typewriter properly, he ran it into the ground.

Question: What is the meaning of "ran it into the ground"?

Student's answer: Put it in a hole in the dirt.

Your reply, if the student can't evaluate his answer:

Let's see: Does it make sense to put a typewriter into a hole in the ground? What would happen to it? [See item 1 below.]

Then too, would you actually *run* to put it in the ground? [See item 2 below.] No, take my word for it. The expression "to run something into the ground" means to use it so hard and so incorrectly that it is ruined, useless. Going back to the text, does this meaning make sense? The text would then say that because he didn't know how to use the typewriter or take care of it, he ruined it.

Now, with this meaning, do the two parts of the sentence make sense together? [See item 3 below.] Does the sentence agree with what we know goes on in reality? [See item 4 below.]

Note that in this discussion, you have given the student four of the expectations that you use to judge whether you are reading the text correctly and getting the right answers to questions about it. They are:

1. The author's ideas must make sense individually.

2. Every single one of the author's ideas must be used—no omissions are allowed.

3. The ideas the author presents in sentences are usually consistent with each other. Each sentence is consistent with the ones that precede and follow it.

4. In nonfiction and realistic fiction, these ideas must agree with our experience in the outside world.

You discuss the answer to each question in order to help the pupil develop a more helpful set of expectations about written communication. You then show him how to use these expectations so that he can independently tell if he understands it correctly.

The technique you use to do all this is simple. You ask the student the meaning of something in the text. To help him decide if his answer is right, you substitute his meaning in the text for the term that was explained. You then see if the "new" sentence meets your expectations for printed materials. Sometimes you see if the "new" sentence makes sense with the sentence before or after it.

Occasionally, be sure to ask the pupil to tell you how he knows that his answer is right, when in fact it is. Don't only ask him to prove the correctness of answers that are wrong. If you do, the pupil will soon learn that if you ask him about it, the answer must be wrong. You don't want that, because then the pupil doesn't need to develop or use an awareness of the characteristics of sensible material to help him decide if he's getting the right information. Instead, he's using a signal from you. Further, that's the reverse of how we comprehend in real life. First we test an answer. Only after we've tested it can we tell if it's right or wrong, and whether or not it should be changed.

From time to time you will have to tell a student the meaning of a term such as "to run something into the ground." You do that because he needs to know what people mean when they use that expression. You also want him to learn how to be more independent and active in comprehension. Avoid the trap of saying "Learn it because I say so." That discourages independent thinking. It isn't the real reason he should learn it.

What You Can Expect

Your student will learn to use appropriate internalized expectations slowly. For older students it can take a year or two, doing two lessons a week. If I knew a quicker way to solve the problem, I'd share it with you. Nor do I know of anything which is more important or necessary to do for the youngsters who need Structured Comprehension.

Some processes are gradual. Getting students to apply this active "I'm trying hard to find the meaning" approach to their reading of more than one sentence at a time, is one of them.

When my remedial groups could do five perfect papers in a row, I would come in and make a big fuss about how far my students had come. I would tell them that they were now ready to do a much more difficult and mature kind of task (often to the accompaniment of quiet groans). From now on, we were not going to read *one* sentence at a time before answering questions, we were going to do *two* sentences. I was not surprised to have the scores drop down to about as low as they were originally. This continued for a lesson or two, but then the scores started to climb again. When my groups could get five perfect papers in a row on two sentences, I felt it was important to make the same kind of congratulatory fuss again, and we would move up to doing three sentences at a time. Again, the scores would tumble for a short time, but we would push right on until, adding one sentence at a time, we could do five or six sentences at a time and get five consecutive papers completely right. Then I switched the focus of our activity to a higher level comprehension skill, main idea. (See Chapter 5.)

It would be good if your student automatically carried over his Structured Comprehension skills when he did other kinds of comprehension work. He doesn't for quite some time, unless you constantly remind him that he should.

Teaching my pupils how to organize a notebook and keep records of their own work was, for a variety of reasons, an important part of what I tried to do. For one thing, these were among the most disorganized children in the whole school. If they had a completely blank notebook, they could do September tenth's lesson on the fifty-sixth page of it, September eleventh's on the twenty-fourth page, September twelfth's on the third page, and so forth. So I always insisted that they put their name and other identifying information on the first page and then use and date each succeeding page for each succeeding assignment. Left to their own devices, these children do not find their notebooks are useful study aids. Not only are their note-taking techniques usually quite poor, but as I have just explained, they have no way of knowing what sequence their notes should follow. So I went around the room daily and made sure that the notebook pages were being used in order.

Showing Progress to Students

The last few pages of the student's notebook were reserved for record-keeping, which I felt was probably as important as anything else I did with these pupils. The last page of the notebook was headed "One Sentence Structured Comprehension." The lines below each contained the date of each assignment and the score earned. This page then told us when we could go on to doing two, three, etc. sentences at a time. Each time we made those moves we changed the heading to "Two, Three, Four, or Five Sentence Structured Comprehension." Every few weeks I would have everyone turn to the record page, but instead of just having the pupils record the day's date and score, I would look over each notebook and be surprised, pointing out how the student's record proved he could do things that he could not do before. Notice, I never told them that they were very bright or very good comprehenders. Such messages would run counter to the views they had of themselves and would therefore have been rejected. But their record-keeping pages showed them evidence they could not deny—they had made progress, they had moved from being less capable to being more capable, and they could have hope.

Sometimes people wonder if their pupil needs Structured Comprehension because he gets some of the answers right when he first starts the process. Two issues need to be dealt with before this question can be answered. Would the pupil have decided who the pronouns stood for, or which definition of a word applied in this sentence, if you hadn't asked him? If not, he needs this work. Secondly, look at his wrong answers. If they were not tested against valid expectations, that is, they don't make sense in this context, then your pupil needs Structured Comprehension.

However, Structured Comprehension is not a panacea for all comprehension problems. If your student reads easy material and knows what its sentences say, but can't figure out the main idea of a paragraph, or what mood it suggests, or what is likely to happen next, then Structured Comprehension won't be of any help.

The next chapters deal with these problems.

CHAPTER 5

"Studing my notes is like memorizing the telephone book!"

What This Complaint Really Means

Literal comprehension is only a beginning. Full comprehension demands more than understanding individual sentences and the connections between them. It demands that the reader see the relationship of these sentences to some larger purpose the author has. Here's an example:

The invention of the cotton gin made great changes in the economy of the South. Originally, the South grew very little cotton, because it was very expensive to remove the seeds from it in order to make it into cloth. Then Eli Whitney invented the cotton gin, which quickly and cheaply removed the seeds. The cost of the cotton cloth now dropped sharply, which made it possible for many more people to use it. The demand for cotton cloth increased greatly. To meet this demand a large part of the southern economy now turned to raising cotton.

There is nothing about the appearance of the sentences in the previous paragraph that makes any one of them look more important than the others. But the first sentence, "The invention of the cotton gin made great changes in the economy of the South," is the most important one, the paragraph's main idea. That is, each of the paragraph's other sentences only explain or illustrate that main idea. The student who doesn't understand the relationship of the main idea to the rest of the paragraph is in trouble. To him all the sentences in the paragraph are of equal importance. When he reads and studies material that way it *is* like memorizing the Manhattan telephone book —and who can successfully memorize millions of unimportant, unrelated facts?

Let's put it another way. You are going to somebody's house for Thanksgiving dinner. The directions you are given contain six steps. Considered alone, each step has little or no significance. It must be seen in relation to the other steps. However, the only reason those steps exist is because they help you to achieve your main idea, getting to that house for dinner.

To get the message that the author intended us to get (or to "comprehend the passage"), the reader must:

a. understand each sentence;

b. relate it to the sentences that surround it;

c. assign a relative importance to every sentence, which depends on what it contributes to his understanding of the main idea.

Not only does good comprehension demand this process, but the process itself helps us to remember the material better. Near the beginning of Chapter 12, under the heading "How Can Your Student Learn More Effectively?" you will find an experiment (see pages 187–188). It will tell you whether your student is better at remembering information that is related or unrelated. Whether you do the experiment now or when you read Chapter 12, please be sure you do it. It makes a very important point.

Many students don't understand that each paragraph is written around one main idea. Simple though this concept is, it's a very difficult one to teach some people. It's so far removed from the experiences they have as they read, that it's often pointless to tell them that every sentence in a paragraph supports one major idea. Most of us hold on to our present ways of doing things and don't welcome a new approach, even when we finally see that what we've been doing up to now is wrong.

With many students, it's necessary to teach this concept gradually and slowly. You can't teach them the abstract principle "All or almost all paragraphs are organized around one main idea." Instead, surround them with a set of experiences that gradually build this concept in a number of different ways, and keep this up until they grasp it and begin to look for the main idea themselves in what they read.

However, if your student doesn't know what each individual sentence says, and that each sentence is connected to the ones before and after it, then you shouldn't be working on main ideas with him. He isn't ready to take this next important step. You'll be giving him tasks at which he can't hope to succeed, and he doesn't enjoy failing any more than you do.

In all the work I have done with very weak students, I make sure, especially at the beginning, to ask the pupil to do work in which he's almost certain to succeed. I supply enough limits and guidelines so that with my emotional support, he is willing to use his judgment just a bit more than he usually does, and he gets the right answer. After seeing that he can do that and be successful at it over and over, he becomes comfortable with that kind of task. After pointing out that this represents an advance over what he could do before, I pull away just a little bit more of the guidelines, making the task a bit harder. That is, I change the task so that he has to use a bit more judgment, and I give him enough emotional support so that he can get it right. When he consistently gets it right at this level, I point out the progress he has made, pull away a bit more, and so on. The object always is to increase the student's self-confidence so that he will be willing to use his own judgment and understanding often, and rely less on guessing and "I don't know" responses.

Techniques for Teaching Main Idea

How do we decrease structure while working on main ideas? This next technique is one of my favorites. From a social studies book I pick a paragraph that is well-organized. I write its main idea on the board as follows:

I. The three causes of the Civil War were:

   A.

   B.

   C.

I tell my students to copy this outline form on the appropriate page in their notebooks exactly as I have written it on the board. Then I check to see that they have done so. Next they read the paragraph to find the three causes, and fill them in, briefly but clearly, in the appropriate places. If, when the work is done, there is some disagreement, we discuss it and agree on the right answers. If the work is done correctly I show that I'm pleased, and give the student more practice in it until I see that he can usually manage this task independently. My student is ready to go to the next step when he can do four or five lessons in a row without any major problem.

Then I announce that the pupil is now ready to graduate to a more difficult task. From now on, I write the main idea, as before, but don't tell how many details to list under it. The pupil reads the paragraph and we decide together how many details should be noted in support of that idea. This is what I mean when I say I pull away a little bit of structure whenever the pupil shows me he can probably manage without it. Again, when the pupil does five good lessons in a row, I compliment him and say that he is ready to advance to a more mature stage. This time, the student decides without any help from me how many details should be written under the major idea I have supplied.

By this time the youngster has usually told me: "I know where you get the main idea that you write first for every paragraph. It's usually the first sentence of the paragraph."

That's fine. It shows that the student has begun to actively observe what goes on. Shortly after this, I announce another change in procedure. I will no longer write the major idea for the student. Now he and I will choose it together. In the next step I ask the student to find the main idea for himself. The student is left to do the entire task independently.

In addition to using this kind of lesson to teach the main idea concept, I intersperse several others, using different techniques. I believe this multi-faceted approach to comprehending the main idea is the most effective one.

Occasionally I use main idea exercises in workbooks, such as *Reading for Meaning,* by Guiler and Coleman. This book gives a half-page passage, which is usually quite interesting to read. The passage is followed by various kinds of exercises. One is a main idea multiple-choice exercise, another asks the student to pick a title for the passage, which is a similar task.

Another method I use for practice in finding main ideas involves newspaper articles. Cut off the headlines from three stories and put them in a separate pile. Ask the student to read the articles and then match the headlines to the stories. Make sure that all the articles are of the same column width, or else the student can match the article with its headline on the basis of their physical size, rather than on their meaning. You can avoid that problem by writing the headlines on slips of paper.

You can also take simple cartoons and other illustrations and separate them from their captions. The student is given three of each and is asked to match each cartoon or illustration with the correct caption. The captions should be reasonably good main idea statements. You can write your own if need be. One good thing about this technique and the one mentioned above is that you have so much freedom in the articles you select. At the beginning when your student may find the task quite difficult, you should select three articles that discuss three completely different subjects, to make the task easier. Later, when your student develops skill, you can make the exercise more difficult by selecting three different accounts of the same event.

I also use diagrams. These are particularly useful because, according to experimental evidence, people tend to select the wrong main idea in consistent ways. Thus John tends to get the nature of main ideas slightly wrong. Mary tends to overgeneralize them, saying that they cover more information than the author intended them to. Bill tends to take only a small piece of the main idea. So use the diagram technique which I'll describe shortly if you notice a consistent kind of error in your pupil's responses.

Let's assume that you've read the following paragraph about the nose. (Try to use passages that are no bigger than a half-page for this work. If the article is longer, the lesson will take too long.) Ask the pupil to read the passage and suggest a number of main ideas that he thinks might be considered. Then diagram the answers.

Here is a sample paragraph, followed by a group of possible main ideas for it, and a diagram of these ideas.

The nose performs several important services. Although it and the mouth take life-giving air into our bodies, we should breathe only through the nose. It strains small particles out of the air, so that they do not block the tiny passages into the lungs. The nose also filters out many of the air's germs before they can do harm. Further, it has an elaborate device to warm or cool the air we breathe so that it is closer to the temprature of our bodies. And, of course, the nose enables us to smell gases and liquids. The sense of smell is very important, because it gives us information that our eyes and ears cannot tell us.

Here are some of the suggestions students might make in trying to find the main idea of this paragraph, which is that the nose has five important functions.

1. "It's about the nose." This answer is unsatisfactory, because it's too vague to tell you what you need to know when you read the paragraph. The main idea must tell more clearly what the paragraph says about the nose. For example, does it discuss its size or color? Obviously not, so

what does it discuss? Use the five *w*'s to make a vague main idea more concrete. Tell *w*ho or *w*hat the paragraph talks about, *w*hen or *w*here these conditions are true if these are important, and *w*hat is told about the subject of the discussion. It's helpful to state this information in one or two sentences.

2. "The nose takes in air." This is one of the ideas of the passage, but most of the paragraph deals with other things.

3. "The nose kills all the germs in the air." This, like item 2, doesn't describe what the whole paragraph is about. In addition, it isn't exactly what the paragraph says. Correct this statement by comparing it to what the paragraph does say.

4. "We smell with our noses." True, but again, the main idea includes everything in the paragraph, not just one part of it.

If the pupil consistently chooses a main idea that is inaccurate, or too vague, or only a piece of what the paragraph is about, use the diagram to help him correct this tendency. Here's how to do it.

Draw a large circle, which represents either all the possible answers or a too-vague answer to the question: "What's the main idea of this passage?" As you get each suggestion for the main idea, draw it in an appropriate area in the diagram and label it. When each of the details has been put in, put an overall heading over them that binds them all together. (In this case, we used "The Nose Has Five Functions.") The idea that binds together all of the less important details must be the main idea. When this has been completed, show the pupil what his original response was on the diagram, and how he has to change his thinking about main ideas (either be more accurate, or take in more than one detail, or don't overgeneralize) in order to do the job better.

Main Idea Diagram

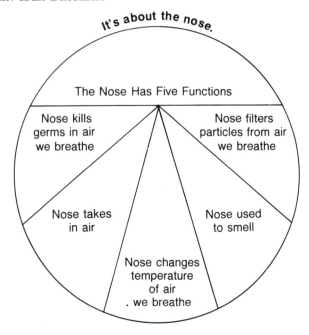

As in the work on Structured Comprehension, encourage the student to reason out the right answers himself, since he must eventually learn to do so without your help. Contribute explanations to these discussions only when you see that if you don't make an important point, your pupil won't pick it up. Once in a while, in a discussion about which statement best sums up the author's main thrust, it becomes clear that you won't convert a die-hard holdout to the correct answer. Then I use a method I call "the tourniquet." This is a very powerful technique and needs to be used only a few times to show even slow pupils the relationship the main idea has to the rest of the paragraph.

Let's assume that you can't convince a student that the main idea of the paragraph was that Fred couldn't buy a shirt he wanted. On a sheet of paper, briefly write the main ideas that have been suggested next to each other on a horizontal line. Now number and read each sentence of the text, one at a time. Write the number of each sentence under every main idea which that sentence supports. After doing this for each sentence, you will see only one of the main ideas suggested was supported by every sentence in the passage. That must be the correct one, because that's how main idea is defined. I've never had a student who was not convinced of the right answer by this demonstration. After seeing "the tourniquet" used, many students have said to me: "Now, for the first time, I see what 'main idea' is all about!" And, as I tell my students, this is an easy trick they can use themselves, once they have seen it done a few times. Here is what a typical paragraph and tally sheet would look like, after we finish our analysis of it.

1. What a beautiful shirt! **2.** The colors and the pattern were just right! **3.** With a dark blue tie, it would be perfect with his new suit. **4.** However, the store didn't have it in his size. **5.** The clerk checked thoroughly, but his size was not there. **6.** Disappointed, Fred left the store, empty-handed.

Main Idea I	*Main Idea II*	*Main Idea III*
It was a beautiful shirt.	They didn't have the shirt in his size.	Though he wanted the shirt, he couldn't buy it.
1	4	1
2	5	2
		3
		4
		5
		6

Some words of caution about all main idea exercises. Before you ask a student to find the main idea of a paragraph, please read it in advance and make sure it has a main idea, whether stated or unstated. I am not being funny. Sometimes an author writes a perfectly good paragraph, but an editor decides that the printed page will look too densely packed. In order to get more white space on the page, he will cut a well-constructed paragraph into smaller paragraphs. The only way to avoid this problem is to be sure to examine in advance the paragraphs you expect to use, and reject the ones that are unsatisfactory.

If you use main idea exercises in workbooks, look them over in advance too. I occasionally find that none of the multiple-choice answers offered really fits. As a result, I am unable to support any of them in the discussion that follows, and my students flounder. Perhaps the paragraph that appears in the workbook by itself originally came between two other paragraphs. When all three paragraphs are read together, the main idea of our middle paragraph has a particular emphasis, since it must be a bridge between the other two paragraphs. But left by itself, as it is presented to us in the workbook, that emphasis may not be evident in any of the multiple-choice answers offered. Another explanation is that some workbook publishers hire people to write materials who have varying amounts of ability. In any case, if the exercise doesn't have an answer you feel you can defend adequately, it's a poor one for you to use in tutoring.

Many writers have noted that in more than 90 percent of paragraphs, the main idea will appear in the first sentence. Most of the rest of the time it will appear in the last sentence. In the remaining few cases, the main idea will not be stated or will be found in one of the other sentences. I'm not sure that these figures are right, but certainly their fundamental thrust is. However, don't teach your pupil to recognize the main idea by its physical position. He needs to understand the relative importance of each of the paragraph's ideas, and how they are connected to each other. If he can get the main idea mechanically, without getting such understanding, he really knows a lot less about what the paragraph says.

Books provide many aids to readers who are main-idea-conscious. Often chapter titles are quite explicit in telling you the major areas about which you will be reading. The boldfaced titles and phrases sprinkled through a chapter also can be helpful in telling you what to look for. Teach your student to use all these aids, once he understands the significance of main idea.

I've helped many children to find main ideas as they read and study. As a result, they understand reading material better and get improved marks. After they learn how to search for main ideas and how to connect the main ideas of the paragraphs to see how they support the main idea of the chapter, they often spend less time in reading and studying. I know how helpful this teaching is because I went through this whole struggle myself.

I received my bachelor's degree at a tough, competitive school. We had frequent, detailed, difficult exams. I hadn't yet learned to study in the ways I've suggested in this chapter, so I watched with dismay as I saw my notebooks pile up page after page of closely written "details" in each subject. When exams came, I was beside myself. The mass of disconnected and apparently unimportant details I had to memorize was overwhelming. There was no way I could possibly remember all of those bits of information. I tried but I could never memorize a huge notebook full of notes, so exams always made me very anxious, and I never got grades as good as I should have. What was worse was that I forget everything I learned within a day or two after the exam. Was this what a college education was supposed to be?

I knew something was wrong. I just had to learn another way to approach my schoolwork. When I prepared for exams with friends, I saw that the students who really knew the material had a different, better way of reading and studying. It took me quite a while to figure out how they did it. "Trial and error" is a slow, painful way to learn. But once I learned to use main ideas as a way to organize what I read, I no longer became so terribly anxious about taking notes, or studying them. I answered essay questions on tests much better because they asked if I recognized the central trends in the material and could provide the details that supported them, which is exactly what reading for main ideas had helped me to do. It even helped me to do better on short-answer tests. I could carry away information that was important to me, remembering it long after the day of the test if I wanted to. I knew that I controlled the situation now—it didn't control me. This study technique really paid off for me, and it will for your student too.

CHAPTER 6

"Of course I know what that word means. It's ... uh ..."

The Value of a Large Vocabulary

Everyone agrees that it's good to have a bigger vocabulary. After all, most of us feel that a large vocabulary is a sign of intelligence. Studies tell us that the more words a person knows, the more probable it is that he has a good education, a high salary, and a prestigious job. Certainly everybody should be alert to the meanings of the words that are being used around him. And there is no question that a good vocabulary is important for students who want to do well on achievement tests and the College Boards.

What Can We Do About It?

How can we increase the number of word meanings available to a high school youngster? First, let's see what he needs to know. He meets many words every day—in reading, tests, and other materials, in lessons and talk that he hears, in the entertainment he enjoys. He knows the meaning of many of those words, but certainly not of all of them. The more of them he knows, the better he understands what's going on around him, how to solve the problems he meets, and how to enjoy what the world has to offer. The more word meanings he knows, the better he's able to discuss and describe, to make his own ideas clear to others.

There's another advantage to studying the words a student needs to know. He'll actually use those words, and that will help him to remember them better.

What can we do to help expand a student's vocabulary? One of the things we all remember is being sent home to memorize the definitions of a long list of words. Most of us forgot the meanings of the words right after the test (and sometimes before) and hated the task. We certainly can't stuff the meanings of a large number of words into people's heads quickly. But we can and should do two other things to help improve vocabulary. One is to change the student's attitude toward vocabulary, so that when we are no longer with him, he will continue to learn the meanings of new words. The second is, since we can only teach a relatively small number of words, the words we teach should be genuinely useful to the student.

Making Words Interesting and Enjoyable

Let's talk about attitudes toward vocabulary first. I delight in bringing the wonder and fascination of words to even the weakest students. I find that students who learn to enjoy words become more curious about them and get a bang out of discovering the meanings of the new words they meet. They no longer regard new vocabulary as though it were medicine—that stuff you have to take even though it tastes awful "because it's good for you." I show them that this stuff really tastes good. I've learned to do this gradually, with short discussions and exercises. There are, in addition, many opportunities to get this idea across to your student when the family is together, outside of tutoring time.

Since every student has one, let's talk about last names. They are a relatively recent development in the history of mankind. One group of last names developed because in any town, many people had the same first name. To indicate which person he meant, the speaker gave the first name and some idea of how the person was related by blood to other people. "I was talking to John yesterday." "Which John?" "I meant John, Jack's son." Soon "Jack's son" became "Jackson." Like most things that serve a useful purpose, it was retained. In some places, a brother and sister would have to have different last names. Kristin could be Lavran's daughter (Lavransdatter), but her brother obviously couldn't be anyone's daughter, at least until sex-change operations began a few years ago.

Another common group of last names also arose out of the need to identify which of several Freds or Johns you were talking about. Frequently, people said, "Fred the carpenter," using the person's job to identify whom they meant. Thus, a look at any telephone book listing includes names such as Archer, Baker, Butcher, Butler, Carpenter, Cook(e), Farmer, Fiddler, Miller, and Tailor (Taylor). Almost all of these are easy to recognize as occupation names, to people who speak English. Many more people have last names that stand for occupations in other languages. Thus in German, Bauer means peasant or farmer. Zimmerman means carpenter. Portnoy, Schneider, and del Sarto mean tailor in Russian, German, and Italian, respectively. Chevalier and Cavaliere mean horseman in French and Italian. Kushner and Sapozhnick mean milliner and cobbler in Russian. The Japanese name Shiota identifies a salt-field worker. The list could go on and on.

Still another series of last names arose because they identify a person by telling where he lived. Warshawer, Moskowitz, De Paris, London, and Berliner are obvious European examples. In Japanese, Ohashi, Nakahashi, and Kohashi are last names that mean big bridge, middle or medium bridge, and small bridge, respectively. The names Oyama, Nakayama, and Kohama mean big mountain, middle or medium mountain, and small mountain, while Takayama means high mountain. In Russian, the name Gorodski identifies a city-dweller.

The point is that last names have interesting origins. Everybody has a last name that may have an interesting story behind it.

Many words and phrases have fascinating origins. Have you

ever wondered where the word *dandelion* came from? Centuries ago, Frenchmen returning from journeys to other lands tried to describe to other Europeans some of the remarkable animals they had seen. In trying to describe how fierce the lion was, they would pluck a long green leaf from the field on which they stood and, pointing to it's large, saw-toothed edges, would say: *Voilà! Les dents du lion!* Which meant, "There they are! The teeth of the lion!"

The drug belladonna is used to open the pupil of the eye. Since large pupils were considered to be very attractive by the Italians, you will not be surprised to learn that the drug name means "beautiful woman."

Many expressions have interesting origins too. "Let's get down to brass tacks" is an expression that developed early in our country's history. Prices were not marked on items in the stores. A housewife and a storekeeper might engage in a great deal of bargaining before they finally agreed on the price of a piece of cloth. Only after such an agreement was reached would the cloth be measured and cut. But yardsticks were handmade and expensive. A storekeeper opening a new shop would borrow a yardstick and place it on his counter, then drive brass tacks into the counter at both ends of the yardstick. The yardstick was returned to its owner and the light-colored brass tacks remained in the dark wood of the counter as a permanent yardstick. So after all the bargaining and other preliminaries were over, "Let's get down to brass tacks" meant that now the deal could be consummated. The purpose for which the two people had originally gotten together could now be realized.

Another fascinating expression is "He has too many irons on the fire." The original form undoubtedly referred to "She." Housewives, before electricity and electric irons, used heavy flatirons. These were heated on top of a woodburning kitchen stove. However, the flatirons got cold very quickly as they were used in the ironing process. So the housewife kept a number of flatirons heating on the stove. As each cooled, she put it back on the stove to reheat, and picked up a hotter one. A very quick, efficient housewife prided herself on working so rapidly that she needed a large number of flatirons heating on the stove to ensure that she always had one hot enough to use. If she was too proud, she had too large a number of irons heating. As a result, some of them got too hot and scorched the clothes when she used them. Thus the expression says that someone who tries to do too much, or too many things at one time, often ends up ruining the work.

Word games also help students discover how enjoyable words can be, but these games, or discussions about interesting word origins, should take no more than five minutes in any given lesson. They are useful as lesson starters, or as a break between two more difficult parts of a lesson, or if you want to end the tutoring with a bit of fun.

One game I use at such times is "Crazy Mixed-Up Words."

Puzzle	*Solution*
dark or thigl	light
sweet or tebtir	bitter
exit or natrecne	entrance
sad or pypha	happy
loss or tirfop	profit

The student is told that the first word on each line is opposite in meaning to the last one, which is the crazy mixed-up word because its letter order has been scrambled. The student is asked to write each last word correctly by unscrambling it. Even very weak students enjoy this game, which offers enjoyable practice in vocabulary and spelling.

If I have just a spare minute or two, I may offer a word puzzle to my class, for them to do as "homework." Often these puzzles involve the use of a double letter. I may ask them to come in for the next lesson with the name of a common household object that has two *u*'s in a row (that is, with no other letter coming between them). The name I am looking for, of course, is "vacuum cleaner." I may ask them to come in with the name of a common occupation that has three sets of double letters in a row. The answer to that one is "bookkeeper."

Again, these activities should take no more than five minutes. None of them is valuable enough in itself to justify taking more time. However, these activities serve to awaken your student to the thought that words have character and can be a lot of fun—especially if you let your interest and excitement show as you present the information. So you should have enough "words-can-be-fun" material on hand at all times so that you can present it at least once very week or two.

This material is easy to locate at your local library. Look up "etymology" (the study of word origins) in the card catalog; any of the books listed will open the door to hours of enjoyable browsing. Eric Partridge, Edwin Radford, and Wilfred Funk have each written a number of delightful books on word origins. Charles Earle Funk and Charles Earle Funk, Jr., have written some books on word origins, and others on how common phrases and expressions have come about. Just to read their titles is enough to make you want to read the books: *Horsefeathers and Other Curious Words; Heavens to Betsy! and Other Curious Sayings; A Hog on Ice and Other Curious Expressions; Thereby Hangs a Tale: Stories of Curious Word Origins.* C. T. Onions (a name to make one shed a tear) is the author of a more scholarly work, *The Oxford Dictionary of English Etymology.* A book that does not list an author is *Picturesque Word Origins,* published by G. & C. Merriam. Your library catalog's etymology listings will tell you what is locally available.

Here is a technique that improves vocabulary more directly.

Get in the habit of clipping and saving illustrations that you feel will make a deep impression, that will grip your student. Show one of these pictures, and ask what words the picture evokes. Sometimes a picture that I think will make a deep impression makes none, or perhaps overwhelms the viewer, who then finds it difficult to make any response at all. Discard that picture and take another. Be sure to have a number on hand. A good picture is one that brings to mind a large number of individual words. Feel free to add some of the words that this picture brings to your mind too. Write the words down, then look them up. Talk about their meanings, and compare them. What is done with them now depends upon the sophistication and curiosity of the student. If you do no more than was just described, there is a good chance that each of you has learned a few words or more exact word meanings, particularly if there is a bit of discussion about how the picture evoked each word. The point is that words and their definitions will be remembered more easily if they are connected to feelings. Emotions tend to stamp things into memory more sharply.

More sophisticated students can be set to work to discover the differences between words that we generally regard as having the same meaning. *Sick* and *ill* are almost completely interchangeable and suggest a temporary condition. *Sickly*, however, describes a permanent state. *Diseased* is not quite the same as any of the others. It means definitely having a disease; and one can have an upset stomach, for example, and feel sick without necessarily being diseased.

The student should number and list the new words and their definitions in a special section of his notebook. Make sure this is done, because every few weeks you should turn to these pages and show the student how many words he now knows that he didn't know before. This is a great technique for encouraging the pupil to keep up the good work.

In a few days, show the picture again, and ask how many words that describe it the student can remember. Then go back to the vocabulary list for missing words. In the meantime, try to include these words in your conversation. Be quick to praise the student every time he uses one of the words when he talks or writes. His use of the word, besides helping to fix it in his memory, also enables you to see if its meaning has been correctly grasped. I will never forget the pupil who looked up *seething* and then wrote it in a sentence: "The eggs were seething on the stove." *Seething* means "boiling in anger."

This approach can be varied. You can prepare a list of words and a few pictures in advance. Ask the student to tell you which words apply to a specific picture, or to more than one. The student can look up the words he doesn't know. Then, review the words by matching them to appropriate pictures. Of course, all the new words and definitions should be added to the list in the student's notebook.

Learning the Words We Need to Know

Although building attitudes that stimulate the student to enjoy words and "collect" new ones is important, an adequate vocabulary program demands more than that. Every day, all of us meet new words in reading and conversation. We need to know their meanings in order to understand what is going on. The student with below-average vocabulary is at a great disadvantage. He meets a higher number of words whose meanings he doesn't know, and this hurts his comprehension. There are two ways to deal with this problem, and one is much better than the other.

Approach A has an authority select a list of words that he feels the student (and everybody else) should know. The student memorizes the words and their definitions, maybe uses them in sentences, and then gets a test to determine if he knows them. Because most people feel this is an annoying chore, and have no other need to use or know these words, they report that they forget most of the definitions right after the test (if not before).

Approach B makes much more sense. It says that the student should learn the words he needs to know, the words that puzzle him when he reads and hears them. If these words occur in textbooks and classroom explanations, there's a good chance they will appear again and again, blocking comprehension each time.

How should we deal with these words? How we deal with them depends partly on the nature of our student. Some students are quite active and independent. Once they are aware that they have a problem, or that something ought to be done, they need little or no further direction and succeed in solving the problem themselves. Other students are more passive and dependent. They avoid facing problems. If they are made aware that they have a problem, they sit and wait for others to solve it, or to tell them how the problem should be attacked.

Let's deal with the more passive students' problems first. These are people who are quite likely to need a Structured Comprehension program. As you know, such a program constantly ask pupils to define the words and terms used in the sentences they read. When I taught these children I listed each word or phrase that gave difficulty in my own notebook. As soon as I got ten, my next lesson was already prepared for me—almost.

I would list the ten "new" words or phrases we had discussed, together with a brief definition for each one as it was used in our reading. The pupil copied them into a vocabulary section of his own notebook—again, I carefully supervised to make sure that the copying was done accurately, and onto the right pages. This was another reinforcement of the meanings he needed to know to work in his social studies text (if that is the book we were using). Once the copying was done, the notebook was closed, and the definitions on the board were erased, leaving only the original words. (If you are using paper instead of a blackboard, just cover the definitions.) I asked for the definitions of the words or terms again, which served as another reinforcement. Then with those words still in front of us on the board or paper, I gave my students ten sentences, orally and one at a time. Each sentence had a blank in it. Each blank was to be filled with one of the words on the board. This supplied yet another reinforcement, as did the subsequent review and discussion of the exercise.

More active students can be given more responsibility for dealing with their vocabulary problems, but they still need some direction. Some teachers feel that they should preview each of the reading assignments they make, in order to pick out and explain the words that will give their readers vocabulary problems. Before I came to work at Adelphi University, I taught in elementary and secondary schools for seventeen years, primarily in remedial classes. In spite of my best efforts, I always seemed to define the words my classes already knew and bypass the words they did not know. This became such a frustrating experience that I developed a theory to explain it. My theory is that no matter how many or how few words students know, no two students have exactly the same vocabulary. I make this point to establish the following fact: There is no way in the world that you can consistently guess which words need to be defined for any given individual.

But even if there were, I don't think it would be good to do it. Often a student doesn't know the meaning of a word or expression that is used. He needs to know it to understand what's going on. He may be the only one to realize that he doesn't know it. He has to ask himself: "Which meanings don't I know, and what should I do about them?" If we don't instill in him the habit of asking this question, he may never learn to take this responsibility. We will have to stand by his elbow and solve his vocabulary problems for him for the rest of his life. And, as I suggested in the previous paragraph, no one is in as good a position as the reader himself to decide which are the words whose meanings he needs to learn. So what we really need to do is to train the reader so that he is alert to these words and knows what to do about them.

Teaching pupils that it is important to be alert to words that cause gaps in their comprehension because they don't know their meanings is easy enough to do, if you pay a little attention to it. Not only must you *say* that it is important to track these meanings down and fit them back into their sentences, but you must *do* something about it. Show by *your* actions that it is important. This means that every once in a while, when a student completes a reading assignment, you will give him a quiz in which he is asked the meanings of important words and phrases *as they were used by the author*. As an example, if you ask the student "What does the word *nectar* mean?" a correct answer would be "the wine of the gods." However, if the text talked about the nectar that bees collect and your question did not specify that particular context for the word, you still would not know if your student understood the text. In any case, an occasional vocabulary quiz, if it is given by someone who uses it to help the student rather than to trap him, can show the student how important it is to attend to new vocabulary.

As I've said, the new words to be learned should come from the student's classroom texts and discussions, but it is also important to recognize that the words should be studied when they come up, because that is when they are needed. Don't avoid the issue. We are all tempted to avoid teaching a new word from the text to a student who is weak in vocabulary when the word is too long or too technical. You aren't doing the student any favor. The student's ability to identify a process by name can be crucial if that name appears in a test question. If the student needs it now, study it now. Do that instead of asking the student to study a group of words today that he won't find in the text until next month—the more so if there are words in today's assignment (and there probably are) that merit this attention. If in addition to the reinforcement of the meaning caused by hearing and reading those words again, the student uses the words in his own sentences correctly, the words will become even more firmly fixed in his memory.

Let me emphasize here that the words to be studied should not come from lists that other people make up for us because it would be "good," in some nonspecific way, to know these words. The student should not learn words to impress other people. He should learn words that he has a real need to know, or that appeal to him.

Not only whole words and expressions but also needed affixes and roots should be studied. (In the word *insufferable,* "suffer" is the root, while "in" and "able" have been affixed to it, to change the meaning slightly.) When classroom discussions or the text introduce groups of words that share the same roots or affixes, these should be pointed out and their meanings should be discussed. In chemistry, for example, it's very useful to know that "ose" at the end of the name of a substance tells us we are dealing with a form of sugar. The suffix "ase" tells us that the substance is an enzyme.

The Context or the Dictionary?

How should the student discover the meanings of words or terms he needs to know? Experts disagree on this issue. Some believe that the reader should first try to use the setting, or context, in which the word was found. Often it contains enough information to give the reader a fairly good idea of the meaning of the word. Some say the dictionary should only be used as a last resort, when the context is not helpful enough. The argument is offered that most people will not want to interrupt their reading to find a dictionary and use it, so we might as well teach them how to figure out word meanings by using the context as efficiently as possible.

A few experts disagree strongly. They contend that sometimes the context will offer no help. Worse yet, sometimes it only seems to be helpful. The reader is able to figure out an apparently satisfactory meaning and will go on reading, unaware that this was not at all the meaning intended by the author. Thus for years I assumed that *erstwhile* meant "earnest." It seemed to fit that meaning in every context in which I read it. I accidentally saw it in a dictionary one day and was astonished to discover that it meant "former," and that I had been using it incorrectly for years.

On the other hand, the fact that a reader uses the dictionary is no guarantee that he will discover the right answer. Often the dictionary offers many definitions of a word. (My dictionary, by no means a complete one, offers 145 definitions for the word *run.*) Even if it only offers four or five, many readers, unfortunately, do not look for the definition of the word that fits best in the original sentence.

So both the use of the dictionary and the use of the context have their drawbacks. I'm inclined to say: "Let's teach the use of context to help define words and phrases. Let's also teach people to use the dictionary when the context doesn't offer enough helpful information, or when the reader has enough time and willingness to use it." I am unwilling to go along with those who say "Don't use the context at all." I just don't believe that many people will take the trouble to go to the dictionary when the context seems to tell them quickly what the word means. I suspect that we learned most of the words we know without using the dictionary.

So let's teach people how to use the context first, in an organized way. Often the author recognizes that he has used language that the reader is not likely to understand, and explains it directly. "An osteoma is a tumor on a bone, or a tumor of bonelike tissue." "Near the entrance to the harbor was a shoal, or shallow sandbank or bar, slightly below the surface of the water." "Basil (one of many plants that are species of the mint family) is often used to flavor food." "He carefully walked out on the jetty. This was a stone wall built out from the shore to protect against the action of the waves." Thus a student who does not understand a word or group of words should first search the sentence in which it appears; if there is no explanation there, he should go on to the next sentence. There are many other ways in which an author indicates directly to the reader what a given word means.

Although no author can afford to explain every single word or phrase he uses, the reader will often find that he can figure out the meaning, or something close to it, if he tries. "It was a jerry-built house and would not last as long as the others near it." Here *jerry-built* must mean built in an inferior, less permanent way. At other times, the emotional climate of the content gives us a good idea of the meaning of an unfamiliar word or phrase. "Everyone was arguing with somebody else. Some were shouting, while others controlled themselves. Discordance was the order of the day." Here the mood suggests that disagreement would probably be the meaning of *discordance*.

Sometimes the internal parts of the word can be used to help figure out its meaning. Thus *prolocutor* means one who speaks for others. "Pro" means "for," "locution" means "speech," and the ending "or" means a person who does something. To be sure, whenever meanings are found they have to be fitted into the original context, to see if the sentence now makes sense by itself and is consistent with the other sentences that surround it. In any case, students should be given practice in using all of these techniques in figuring out the meanings of words and expressions they are not sure they know. When the words are figured out, a dictionary should occasionally be used to check on the supposed meaning.

And so we come at last to using the dictionary. Nothing looks simpler to the person who thinks he already knows how to do it; nothing is quite so frustrating to the person who does not. And frankly, people who are frustrated and ineffective in using a dictionary simply are not likely to use one. Nowadays, most elementary schools teach children how to use the dictionary. If your youngster didn't learn it, he has a real disadvantage. My own early difficulties with using the dictionary make me painfully aware of that.

I learned how to read without learning the alphabet or alphabetical order. I'm not sure of why or how, but that was the case. As a result, I almost never used a dictionary simply because it took me too long to locate the word I needed. This was true in spite of the fact that every elementary classroom I sat in had a handwriting chart above the blackboard across the front of the room. It showed the letters, alphabetically arranged. It never occurred to me that I could use the handwriting chart to help locate the word I wanted in a dictionary, or to help me learn alphabetical order. The chart had to do with handwriting. Using a dictionary obviously was a problem in a different area altogether, and I just never connected the two. So for years I rigorously avoided using the dictionary. At some point, probably around seventh grade, when it got too inconvenient, I made up my mind to learn alphabetical order.

You might think that my dictionary problems were solved

from that point on, but they weren't. It was not until several years later that I finally noticed and figured out why every dictionary page had two words in boldface type at the very top. These are called guide words. The one on the left was the first one defined on that page, and the one on the right was the last one defined on that page. This made it possible for me to use the dictionary much more efficiently. If the word I wanted fell alphabetically between the two entry words, it was probably defined on that page. If it alphabetically fell before the left entry word it would be on a previous page. If it alphabetically fell after the right entry word it was on a subsequent page. Theoretically I no longer had to fight increasing impatience and frustration as I ran my eye down two columns on each of several pages before I finally located the word. (Of course, if, as occasionally happened, the dictionary didn't list and define my word, I was doubly furious.) In fact, I had so firmly established the habit of checking every word in each column for several pages, that I have to consciously remind myself, even now, to use the guide words.

Habitual use of guide words, however, does not solve all dictionary use problems. I always ask my graduate students: When a word has more than one meaning, how do the dictionary's editors decide the order in which they will appear? Many students raise their hands. One will say that the most commonly used meaning appears first, and the less commonly used meanings follow. At that, several students who had the same idea put their hands down. Others keep their hands up, although they appear to be somewhat less sure of themselves. One of them says, a little hesitantly, that the definitions are given according to the use of the word. Its meaning as a noun is given first, then its use as a verb, and so forth. This causes most of the remaining students to lower their hands, but a few still have their hands up. This group is now quite indecisive. One of them volunteers that the oldest meaning is first, later meanings are next, and the current meaning is given last, isn't that so? The point is that all three groups are right—sometimes. It depends on which dictionary the student looks at. If you assume that the most frequently used meaning is given first when actually the earliest meaning of the word is given first (and that meaning is probably no longer in current use), you may get a wrong impression. So every time you pick up a dictionary you've not used before, spend a few minutes looking at it. It is easy to tell if definitions are listed in accordance with a word's use as a noun, then as a verb, etc. However, if the definitions are not listed that way, refer to the introduction or explanatory notes at the front of the book. There you will learn which way of ordering the definitions the editors have followed. As a matter of fact, it's always a good idea to look at the introductory material and the table of contents. You generally get a lot of useful information, such as how to look up a word when you don't know its spelling, or how to look up an expression or idiomatic phrase. The more you know about the different kinds of help your dictionary can give you, the more likely you are to use it productively.

The most complete and specific discussion of dictionary skills and how to teach them that I know is written by Ruth Horton. It is found on pages 15 to 85 in the *Thorndike Barnhart Beginning Dictionary*. It takes up seventy pages because most of them are devoted to games and exercises that teach specific dictionary skills. Horton is apparently a well-organized master teacher with years of experience. She lists all the basic dictionary skills and tells how to teach each one. If a skill is difficult to teach, she takes it in easy stages and builds it up slowly over a number of lessons and exercises. It is difficult to imagine a problem in using the dictionary that Horton does not show you how to overcome. She gives simple, well-organized lessons and exercises in all the significant dictionary skills.

Horton's list of skills is quite complete. I urge you to read it if you have not done so—it may alert you to problems you might not otherwise suspect your student has.

However, a high school youngster will not be happy to do exercises from a "Beginning Dictionary." Instead use the

Thorndike Barnhart Advanced Junior Dictionary, which was designed for use in junior high schools. Its pages X to XXXIII contain many exercises and explanations that will be useful. Or if you prefer to use a higher level book, use Horton's exercises only as a model, selecting more appropriate words for junior high and high school students. It is *not* a good idea to go through each of the kinds of exercises that the dictionaries suggest, because your student will already know many of the things these exercises are designed to teach. How do you know which ones need to be taught? Just watch your student when he looks up a word. If he gets stumped, figure out which part of the process he needs to learn, and see what exercises Horton uses, or what you can figure out yourself, to teach him. As in anything else you do, you may make mistakes. However, neither you nor your student can realistically expect perfection. If you continue to be sensitive to the academic and emotional needs of your student, the mistakes won't count for much, and the helpful work you do will count for a great deal.

The Thesaurus

Although it's not used as often as the dictionary, the thesaurus is a useful tool too. Someone once said that we use a dictionary when we know the word but don't know its meaning, and we use a thesaurus when we know the meaning but don't know the word. Writers often turn to the thesaurus when they wish to find another word or phrase in place of the one they have been using. Since the thesaurus's primary function is not to define words, it's a good idea to use a thesaurus and a dictionary together.

The grandfather of all thesauri is *Roget's International Thesaurus,* which is not organized like a dictionary. Suppose the student wants to find another word for *broken.* Surprisingly, he starts by going to the *second* half of *Roget's,* which is arranged alphabetically. He looks up *broken,* and finds a number of synonyms (words of similar meaning) listed for it. However, the synonyms have slightly different meanings. Thus, for *broken* he finds *fractured, shattered, splintered, burst, interrupted,* etc. He picks the word that's closest to the meaning he wants, and notes the number next to it. He then looks up that number in the first half of the book, which is arranged numerically. Under that number, he will find a group of synonyms that will closely match the specific meaning of *broken* that he wants. The antonyms (words opposite in meaning) are also listed, under the number just before or just after the number that indicates the synonyms. It will be obvious to anyone who looks at a thesaurus that it is rare to find two words whose meanings are exactly the same, even though they are regarded as synonyms. Though their fundamental thrust may be the same, there is almost always some shade of meaning carried by one but not by the other.

Other thesauri are a bit simpler to use. In these, you simply look up a word that suggests the idea you want. It appears in an alphabetical list, much the way it does in any dictionary. The *Webster's Collegiate Thesaurus,* published by G. & C. Merriam in 1976, gives words it regards as synonyms, related words (not quite synonyms), antonyms, and contrasted words (not quite antonyms), with each of these categories clearly marked.

Enhancing vocabulary is a long-term process. However, devoting even a relatively short time to it can have noticeable results. At the Adelphi University Reading and Learning Disability Center, high school juniors and seniors take a reading improvement course. Each class is tested before and after the instruction, to help determine how much improvement has occurred. Part of that testing measures vocabulary. A recent class's average jumped 1.2 years (and that jump was typical) after only twenty hours of instruction, only a small part of which was devoted to vocabulary. Nor were the students asked to memorize lists of words selected by the teacher. Instead they were taught to be actively involved in searching for the meaning in their reading. That, among other things, involved paying more attention to the meanings of known and unknown words. This suggests that although it would certainly help, a student doesn't have to have a tremendous vocabulary to succeed in school. The disadvantage of poor vocabulary is minimized if the student learns to watch for and master the "new" words that are used in his texts and classrooms. One of our successful students reports, "I no longer let the new words slip by."

Every student can profit by improving his vocabulary. Every student can become more sensitive to the enjoyment words offer. A good vocabulary program helps him to do both.

CHAPTER 7

"Maybe if I took a speed-reading course..."

Of all the areas of reading discussed in this book, reading
speed is most likely to capture the interest and enthusiasm of your youngster. However, when a student complains
that he reads too slowly, he's often unaware that he may have
more basic reading problems.

I always ask the youngster who comes to the Adelphi University Reading and Learning Disability Center: "What do *you*
think is wrong with your reading?" If they are in junior or
senior high school they often reply, "I don't read fast enough."
When I test them, it turns out that almost all of them have real
problems of other kinds—they make decoding errors, they have
vocabulary problems, they have difficulty in focusing their attention on literal comprehension, or they have some other fundamental skills problem. Very, very few of them read too
slowly, in spite of their almost universal complaint. In fact,
many of them actually read too rapidly and don't let themselves come into contact with the ideas behind the words. Apparently they have little insight into what the problem really
is. Why then is this comment about reading too slowly made so
frequently?

These students don't enjoy reading. I think their complaint
really means: "I feel a lot of discomfort when I read. Show me
how to spend less time in contact with reading so that I won't

feel so bad." Bear in mind that these youngsters have been referred to a reading clinic. They have many more fundamental skill problems than the average youngster. I am not saying that nobody ever reads too slowly, but simply that we can't take anyone's word for it when they say that this is their problem.

Suppose someone came to the track coach and said: "Teach me to run faster." First the coach would watch the person run. If, instead of putting each foot forward as he ran, the person put one foot somewhat out to the side, the coach would help the runner correct this problem first, before helping him to run faster. Teaching a person to do something wrong faster is not nearly as good as getting him to do it correctly, and then speeding him up. So the first question that needs answering is, "Is this person a competent reader in the first place?" If the answer is no, we need to find out what fundamental skills need improvement. Here is a brief list of the fundamental reading problems that often need to be solved when a person complains that he reads too slowly, and the chapters in this book that will help you solve them.

Skills	*Chapter*
Decoding	3
Literal Comprehension	4
Grasping Main Ideas	5

Let's assume that your student has no fundamental skill problems, but still reads too slowly. What are the basic principles that control reading speed?

Actually, the reader should have a number of different reading speeds. As he sits down to do a given task, he should consciously select the speed that he will use for it. One determinant is the difficulty of the material. Obviously, easy things can be read more rapidly than difficult ones. That brings us to a fundamental rule: Nothing is more important than understanding what you read. If you read material so fast that you don't understand it adequately, what is the point of reading it?

In addition to how hard the material is to read, another factor that determines the reader's pace should be his purpose in reading the material. If he is reading it only for his own pleasure, he can read it as rapidly as he likes, understanding and appreciating it as much or as little as he wants to. On the other hand, if he is going to take a rigorous, searching examination on the text in order to get a license and a job, he will have to read it more slowly in order to understand and learn as much of it as he can.

Unfortunately, there is a personality factor that affects reading speed. Some people find it difficult to take shortcuts or to change the way they do things. They are not comfortable unless they work in a painstaking way that leaves no stone unturned, no word unread. They are afraid that if they leave out a word, it will be just the one they need most. Although these people are sincere in wishing that they could read faster, they have a hard time changing the pace at which they read. But even they can improve their reading speed if they have a really strong desire to do so. For instance, if reading faster would enable them to get their work done on time, they may be motivated strongly enough to improve their reading speed, but it will not be easy.

The sophisticated reader uses several reading speeds. He sizes up each reading task and selects the fastest pace that will enable him to meet his purpose for reading it. Sometimes that "fastest pace" will have to be quite slow. In any case, the speed is determined by that reader's need to understand the material, rather than by a table that tells how fast the average person can read.

Reading for Pleasure

Are there times when we shouldn't try to speed up our reading? Yes. Some material is so hard that we can't read it rapidly. Similarly, some purposes for reading make it impossible to read rapidly.

Sometimes we read a passage just to enjoy it. The more

carefully we read it, the more enjoyment it yields. Slow and even repeated readings when we are relaxed and receptive trigger new associations to the material. These make it much more meaningful or enjoyable to us. Speeded reading robs us of these possibilities. We rush through the text and limit our efforts to finding out what the author said. We screen out our own responses to the material—they take too much time.

Perhaps the most effective statement on trying to speed up reading for appreciation was made in an editorial in *Saturday Review* some years ago. Tongue in cheek, the writer described a tape recorder that would play all nine Beethoven symphonies for the listener in ten minutes. It would be possible to accelerate the playing of the Beethoven symphonies to a lesser degree. The listener could hear if each symphony had four movements or five, how many musical themes Beethoven introduced, how he varied each one, and so forth. The listener could count the various components of the symphony and could describe the mechanics by which it was put together. But if all his effort goes into analyzing the music while rushing through it, none of it is going into feeling the music's emotional message. Furthermore, if the listener speeds up the music, he changes its emotional impact. After all, is it still a funeral dirge if it's played at two or three times its original pace?

Some of our great authors took years and years to reach their insights into human nature, and the events that shape our lives. These ideas are expressed in their books. You need to read slowly to savor their efforts.

Critical Reading

Sometimes we read controversial material. In responding to it we need to take the time to answer such questions as:

1. Which of the author's statements are facts and which are opinions?

2. Is what the author says true? Logically sound?

3. Do other writers give additional information on the subject?

4. Are the writer's values and goals the same as mine?

5. Are his arguments good reasons for me to change my mind or behavior?

Answering these questions can be important and takes time. That time is not likely to be spent when the reader's emphasis is on reading rapidly.

How Fast *Do* You Read?

Albert Harris, a prominent authority in reading, believes that most people can increase their reading speed by 25 to 50 percent without losing comprehension. Do you want to know if your youngster is one of these? Here's some information that will enable you to find out. However, use it with judgment.

1. Don't be concerned about the student's reading speed if he is not an average or better than average comprehender.

2. Start by timing him in the kind of material he wants to read faster. The first time you do this is very important. Get an accurate picture of his present reading rate so that later you can show him how much progress he has made in speeding up. So, the first time, don't let him know you are timing him. It's a rare person who doesn't speed up when he knows he's being timed.

3. Let him read at least a few hundred words silently in each selection while you time him.

4. Check his reading rates in easy and hard materials, unless you are only concerned about his reading rate in one of them.

5. Count the words in ten lines of print. Divide that number by ten to find the average number of words per line. Multiply the number of lines he read by the number of words per line to find how many words he read. Divide the number of words read by the number of minutes he took to read them. To do this, round off the seconds to decimal fractions of a minute, as shown below.

No. of seconds	Round off to
0–7	0
8–22	.25 min.
23–37	.50 min.
38–52	.75 min.
53–60	1 min.

If the youngster took three minutes and ten seconds to read a passage, divide the number of words read by 3.25 minutes. If he took four minutes and forty seconds, divide the number of words by 4.75 minutes. This division tells you the number of words read per minute.

6. Be sure that the student understood the material adequately. If he read it too fast to understand it, his problem is not that he reads too slowly. If he answers multiple-choice questions on the material, he should get at least 70 percent right without looking back. If he summarizes the passage he read, the summary should include most of the important ideas in it.

7. If the student's reading rate was slower or faster than the rates indicated below (say by 50 percent or more), try him on other passages in the same kind of material. He may have read an atypical passage.

8. Use the suggested rates (below) carefully. Use the higher end of each range for really good students, and the lower end for students not as good.

9. Be flexible. The figures below are rough estimates. Reading rates within 25 percent of the ones below may be regarded as normal, if comprehension is adequate.

10. The person who wants to increase his reading speed should be concerned with how much faster he is reading now than he read before. This is more meaningful than whether or not

he catches up to the so-called average reader. After all, the reader's personality, which is not easy to change, has a lot to do with how rapidly he reads.

Reading authorities are in general agreement about the following figures. Please bear in mind that these figures come from observing the reading of other students and are only more or less accurate. The student can use the following table to see approximately how his rates compare with the rates of others.

Reading Rate
(Words Per Minute)

100–150 wpm or less	Really difficult material (e.g., science or math)
200–250 wpm	Moderately difficult material (e.g., history)
250–350 wpm	Easy-to-understand material (e.g., current fiction)
400–500 wpm	Getting the drift of easy material.

Unfortunately, most high school students use only one rate, no matter how difficult the material is or what their purpose is in reading it—between 200 and 250 words per minute.

Harris looks at reading speed differently. He says that a person's normal reading rate is about two-thirds of his most rapid rate. When he reads very difficult material, his reading rate drops to less than one-third of his normal rate. Thus if a person's fastest rate is over 450 words per minute, his normal rate would be 300 wpm, and his rate in hard material is less than 100 wpm.

The student is fully justified in trying to increase his reading speed provided that he's a competent reader, and his fundamental purpose for reading doesn't suffer because he's reading too fast. However, reading difficult material, reading for appreciation, and critical reading can be speeded relatively little, and sometimes not at all. Most other kinds of reading can be done more rapidly, with practice.

Techniques that Increase Speed

Scanning and skimming are two reading processes that can be speeded. Scanning is reading to locate the answer to a specific question. (Other writers may give it another definition.) This can be a time-consuming process. First let's note that there is a good chance that the questions in a list follow the order in which the information was presented in the text. Thus if the student reads several pages of text and, on trying to answer specific questions, doesn't remember where an answer is, he will probably be safe in guessing that the answer to the first third of the questions will probably appear in the first third of the passage, and so on. He can also probably assume that the answer to question three, for example, appears in the text soon after the answer to question two, and before the answer to question four.

If the question asks for the year in which a specific law was passed, the pupil quickly looks at that section of the text where he thinks the answer is. Notice, I did not say that he reads it. He is not looking to get ideas or to understand the meaning— he is looking for a date and the name of a law. When he finds either, he reads the sentence that contains it for meaning. He may need to read a few of the sentences that surround this one. But first he only checks to see which sentence or sentences contain the information he needs. The same rules would apply if he were asked to find information about any proper noun (a noun that begins with a capital letter). If this technique doesn't work, he rereads the short section that he believes contains the answer. This time he looks for the same information, but checks to see if it is given indirectly. Thus the question asks, "What year saw the passage of the Smith-Jones Act?" A direct, easy-to-locate answer in the text would be, "The Smith-Jones Act was passed in 1935." A more indirect statement might be, "A new president was elected in 1932. Three years later, a law was passed which cut off the importation of iron and steel. Named after its sponsors, Senators Jones and Smith . . ." If the pupil can't find the answer after a second try, he may look in another section of the text that is more likely to contain the answer. His best bet is to look up the name of the law in the index at the back of the book. A minute spent looking at the beginning page of the index will probably be quite helpful. In many instances this will contain a key that tells which of the cited pages has a definition, a picture, a map, an extended explanation, or some other form of entry.

Another reading activity you can hope to increase in speed without damaging understanding is called skimming. (Again, other authors may give skimming another meaning.) Skimming, unlike scanning, is used to provide general information about a book. A person can skim for two different reasons. In the first instance he wants to know if a book deals with a specific area of information that he needs. Let's say a student is doing a paper on the life of Napoleon. He already has a lot of information, but feels he needs to get more about the time Napoleon spent on Elba. He goes to the library and finds another book on Napoleon. Short of reading the whole book, what can he do to see if it has what he needs?

First he should check the table of contents. This part of the book often lists the major areas discussed, chapter by chapter. Since he knows that history books usually describe what occurred in chronological order, and the exile occurred later rather than earlier in Napoleon's life, he looks at the last third of the table of contents. Sometimes under each chapter title is a brief list of the topics discussed in that chapter.

Often, however, the table of contents lists only chapter titles. These may be symbolic or poetic in nature. In that case, they have little or no meaning until *after* the chapter is read. If that is the case, the student should turn to the index and see if it lists "exile" or "Elba." If it does, he turns to the pages indicated and sees if they contain enough of the information he needs. If there is no index, he uses the technique discussed below.

The second reason to skim is related, but not identical. Sometimes you want to know what specific area of information a chapter (or section of a book) covers, or what point of view is taken by the author. The table of contents sometimes is detailed enough to tell you what is covered in the chapter. The author's point of view is often described in the preface. But if neither of these has helped, you will have to use a technique called surveying. Again, this should take a lot less time than reading the material. With a little practice, students can be taught to survey quite rapidly. Here is the technique, which is used for nonfiction primarily.

As the student surveys a book, he should constantly bear in mind the question, "Is what I want to know likely to be here?"

1. Carefully read the chapter or section title and the paragraphs that introduce that part of the text. They usually tell the reader what topics the chapter will cover.

2. Carefully read the rest of the chapter, up to its concluding paragraph(s), in accordance with these rules:
   a. Read the first sentence of each paragraph; it probably contains the paragraph's most important idea. Much less often, that idea will be found in the paragraph's last sentence.
   b. Carefully but quickly check the meaning of all headings and statements in boldface (heavy) type. These also indicate the areas that will be described.
   c. Carefully examine all illustrations, maps, diagrams, etc., as you go.

3. Read the final paragraphs carefully. They usually review what the chapter has covered. You should now know if that chapter contains the information you want.

Reading Nonfiction Faster

If the material surveyed appears to be useful, read it more carefully. Within reason, you can still speed up this reading. Since understanding is the key to rapid reading, anything that helps you to understand the material more rapidly will help you read it more rapidly. Your survey has already given you the overall plan of the selection. Just *knowing* that plan allows you to read about 25 percent faster, since you already know the important ideas and how they fit together.

In addition to knowing the overall plan, recognize that smaller bodies of information within it are presented in specific patterns or schemes. Recognizing these schemes also helps you read faster and more effectively, because there is a specific reading and study technique for each one. For example, if a passage in a science book classifies the different kinds of insects, the reader recognizes the classification pattern. To learn material written in this pattern, he memorizes the name and definition of the overall group, each category in it, the similarities that unite them, and the differences that distinguish them from each other. His awareness that a specific pattern is used causes him to pick the fastest, most effective way of learning it.

To help you further, here is a group of schemes used by authors to organize their writing. They are used most commonly in social studies texts, although they also appear in many other kinds of writing.

1. Presentation of a lot of evidence to support an opinion, which then follows.

2. The reverse of the previous scheme. Here the opinion is presented first and is followed by the evidence that supports it.

3. A cause-and-effect relationship. The effect, a poor crop, was caused by inadequate rainfall and abnormally hot weather.

4. A compare-contrast situation, in which two people or situations, for example, are discussed. The author tells us how they are similar to and different from one another.

5. An enumeration of events. They can be arranged according to the order in which they occurred, or by some other principle. The reader must discover that principle.

6. A question is asked and is followed by a long answer.

If the student has to do a great deal of reading in subjects besides social studies, H. Alan Robinson's book *Teaching Read-*

ing and Study Strategies lists the schemes by which authors present ideas in those curriculum areas.

It probably seems strange to you that the student who improves his comprehension gets a free bonus of increased speed as a result, even though he makes no attempt to work at speed. But it's true. At the Adelphi University Reading and Learning Disabilities Center, high school youngsters who are at least average students can take a reading improvement course. They work only on comprehension and get no speed-reading training at all. Their reading rates are tested on two different but equivalent forms of the same standardized test. This is done once at the beginning of their instruction and once at the end. The following figures tell what happened to the reading rates of a recent, typical class of fourteen students.

Average rate before instruction	176 wpm
Average rate after instruction	287 wpm
Average increase	111 wpm

Every student's reading rate improved, although, of course, some rates improved more than others. These students averaged a 61 percent increase in reading rate.

Let me repeat an important warning. Nothing, but nothing in reading is more important than understanding. The person who values reading speed to the detriment of understanding will suffer for it. The normal reader can, by scanning, skimming, and noting the author's organizational patterns, hope to increase his reading speed moderately in nonfiction material. As before, how rapidly he reads must be determined by how difficult the material is and the purpose for which he reads it. Texts in mathematics and science can rarely be read at substantial speed if they cover difficult material.

Reading Fiction Faster

Most people can increase their speed in reading fiction. However, the more a reader pushes for speed, the less he can appreciate the pleasures available in the story (which are not necessarily quickly evident), and the less critical thinking he will be able to do about the narrative. These considerations can be very important.

Most traditional fiction follows a standard pattern. The time and place in which the action occurs are established quickly. The protagonists are introduced early, as is the conflict between them. The protagonists' characters are shown by their reactions to the events of the story. These generally start off at a low pitch of excitement. One event leads to the next. Each event intensifies the conflict between the protagonists and makes the final resolution of that conflict more inevitable and necessary. Finally, following the climax of the story, the conflict is settled, and our suspense about it is relieved. The content of each story suggests or directly states a theme—a significant belief the author has about people and events, or about the general conditions that shape our lives, and it, of course, affects the outcome of the story.

The student will need to know all of the preceding information about any traditional fiction read in response to a school assignment.

As he reads, he should push himself to read as rapidly as he can while still trying to grasp the fundamentals of the story's structure. Once he realizes what each part of the story depicts, and that the rest of this part will only elaborate what is already known, the reader can quickly skim the material, paying relatively little attention until a change in the content occurs. The main emphasis for the reader should be the discovery of the story's time and place, the personalities and basic conflicts of the protagonists, and the events that lead into, as well as the resolution of, the major conflict. By focusing attention on this kind of information and paying little attention to the rest of the story, the reader's speed increases, as does his efficiency in grasping the material, and even his understanding of it. For school assignments, knowing the theme is important, and it should be sought after reading the story.

Other Ways to Help Your Youngster Increase Reading Speed

The competent reader who wants to read fiction with more speed and fluency should push himself by reading a lot of easy, enjoyable material as rapidly as possible. In order to read nonfiction more rapidly than he currently does, he should survey the material first. An experiment has shown that after practicing a few times a week for one month, high school students need no more than one or two minutes to survey a chapter in a textbook. Those who do survey in advance spend considerably less time to read the chapter than those who do not, with no loss in comprehension. (See pp. 189–192 on how to survey) In the reading improvement course, after surveying, and reading the material more quickly than usual, the student writes a brief summary of it, and then compares the summary to the text. The object is to read the material as fast as he can, so long as he is still able to write an accurate summary of it. Your student should practice these three steps for nonfiction—surveying, reading, and summarizing—choosing passages of equal difficulty.

If he is timed, he will be more motivated to substantially improve his reading (and comprehension) rate. Often progress is evident in the first lesson, but practice is necessary to improve reading speed and maintain it at a higher level.

Each time I talk about this topic, some members of my audience say: "The advertisements for speed-reading courses make them look so attractive and simple. My child is not self-disciplined. If we pay for a course and he has to go to it regularly, he'll have a better chance of doing the work. And besides, they use machines to help."

You'll be better able to judge the worth of such courses if you know something about the origins of speed-reading, how speed-reading machines work, how nonmachine speed-reading courses work, and what you can expect from them. (One thing you can expect is a bill.)

In the early 1900s, Javal discovered a way to record the eye movements of readers. He found that we glance at each line of print a number of times. The reader's eye takes in a number of letters at each glance or fixation. Obviously, the larger number of letters he takes in per fixation, the fewer fixations he will need to read a line of print, and the faster he will be able to read. In the same way, it's faster to measure a twenty-foot wall with a yardstick than with a six-inch ruler. Javal learned that more competent readers took fewer fixations to get across a line of print than less competent readers. This led to a new approach: You can read faster if you increase the number of letters you take in at a glance, because you will then need fewer glances (fixations) to read a line of print. If you also decrease the time spent on each fixation, you will further improve reading speed. This explanation is simple, logical, and straightforward. It has one other attribute—it's wrong. If it were right, why would the same individual read some kinds of reading matter more rapidly than other kinds? The answer is obvious. The good reader can't let himself read any faster than he can understand the material. If it is difficult to understand, he has to slow down.

In any case, one of three types of machines used to speed read is based on widening and quickening the eye span. The machine, called a *tachistoscope,* flashes words, numbers, or phrases on a screen. The operator of the machine can increase or decrease the number of letters or numbers that will be flashed at any one time. He can also increase or decrease the amount of time that these words or numbers will be visible on the screen—a twenty-fifth of a second, a fiftieth, a hundredth, etc. As an indication of how little the manufacturer understood what was really involved, the phrases flashed on the screen were not meaningfully connected to each other. Work done with this machine, when I last saw it some years ago, disregarded the area of comprehension altogether.

A second type of machine, called the *accelerator,* operates differently. First the individual's normal reading speed is determined, usually using factual material of moderate difficulty. Then a book is placed in a machine. The desired number of words per minute is entered on a dial. When the accelerator starts, an opaque bar moves inexorably down the page. The student has to read the material before the bar covers it at the speed set on the dial. This program has the individual reading continuous, sensible material. When the student finishes reading, he checks his comprehension by answering twenty multiple-choice questions without looking back at the text. This check is a good idea, since the pupil can thus be kept from reading at a speed that is too high for him to comprehend the material. If the reader gets a comprehension score of 70 percent or higher, he tries to increase his reading speed by 10 percent next time he uses the accelerator.

Once, after using this program for several weeks with a group of high school juniors and seniors who were readers of at least average ability, we tired of answering those multiple-choice questions about specific details. I asked my classes to demonstrate their comprehension of the passage by summarizing it in a paragraph. They were quite unable to do it, though many of them were honor students. I drew the conclusion that they had learned by experience that they were going to be questioned only on details, and so read the material with that in mind. They obviously did not comprehend the story—they could report neither what fundamental problem the protagonists had to solve nor how they solved it. In spite of this, the program was encouraging them to read faster and faster.

The third mechanical device used in speed-reading classes is the film. A moving finger of light illuminates the successive words in a printed passage that is projected on a screen. The reader's rate is controlled because he can only read the words while they are illuminated. The projector operator sets the speed of the moving light in accordance with the needs of his students. Many companies market such programs. Some use one projector for a whole class. Others have one projector per student, which allows each student to work at his own pace.

These programs vary widely in the preparation for reading and the subsequent comprehension testing they give the students.

In general, students are initially highly motivated by the machines, although a few are intimidated by the thought that something outside themselves will control their reading rate. I wonder if the enthusiasm of most of the others doesn't come from the mistaken idea that machines will do part of the reading for them. I've observed that students speed up quickly at first, but then they find it increasingly difficult to speed up more, and their enthusiasm drops rapidly.

Other criticisms of speed-reading courses that use machines are more serious. These programs tend to present only one kind of reading material in lesson after lesson, and to explore only one kind of comprehension in the check-up tests. The reader is not being taught to be flexible—to vary his rate in accordance with how difficult the material is, or in accordance with varying purposes for reading it. His only concern is to equal or improve his last reading rate.

Another criticism of these machine programs is that when the machines are taken away, people tend to go back to their former reading speeds. In addition, it has been found that machine programs are not more effective in producing reading-rate gains than nonmachine programs.

One type of nonmachine speed-reading program teaches the reader to follow his fingertip as it sweeps down a page of text. Various finger-sweep patterns are taught. As the student reads faster and faster he is encouraged to use more and more abbreviated sweep patterns. I've talked to a number of intelligent adults who have to read difficult material, and have taken these courses. Their experience is that they help the reader get a quick idea of what the text is about in a general way, but that a reader who has to read and absorb difficult material, or who wants to appreciate and enjoy what he reads, or who needs to critically evaluate it cannot use finger-sweep methods.

If someone you know still insists on taking a speed-reading course, here are some questions for him to consider:

1. Is each applicant tested to see if he is a competent reader before taking the course? Do they refuse to take applicants whose basic skills are inadequate?

2. Do they differentiate between the kinds of reading? Do they say that you should read everything faster and, by implication, at the same rate?

3. Do they point out the disadvantages of speeding up reading for appreciation, or critical reading?

4. Do they say that you should have several reading rates, and tell when each should be used?

5. Do they teach you how to understand what you read faster, or how to make your eyes go over the words faster?

6. Can you talk to former pupils? After they finished the course, did they feel that their improved rates were maintained? If so, what kind of reading were they helped to do? Is this the kind of reading you have to do?

Many of us are astonished by the speed-reading exploits of others. A famous French philosopher and scientist was reported to read really difficult scientific treatises just as rapidly as he could turn their pages. If that makes you shrivel a bit, just remember, any genius who sets his mind to it can do that. But most of us are not geniuses. A more reasonable goal is to try to improve within the limits of our own abilities, without trying to do what genius can do.

CHAPTER 8

"Why don't you _read_ something?"

"Why don't you _read_ something?" is a question many of us ask our kids. If we ask it often, and with annoyance, we're probably not helping our cause. However, it bothers us if our children don't read any more than they have to. And some of them don't even do that.

Why Read Anyway?

Why do we want our children to read? Sometimes it's so that they'll have to stop teasing their sisters, or doing something else we'd rather they didn't do. That may be a good reason for _us_ to want them to read, but it's not a good reason for _them_ to want to read. Sometimes we enjoy reading ourselves, and we want our children to share that pleasure. Sometimes it's because we have a vague feeling that if our children read, their schoolwork will improve. After all, reading is basic to success in almost every school subject.

Perhaps we want them to read because we know that books open the windows of their minds. We feel that people who don't read limit what they know to the things that they can see and experience. Those who do read have no such limits. They can learn and indirectly experience almost everything in the world. So we want our children to be readers.

Some of us feel that television makes it less important to

read, because it too takes us out of our own immediate environment. In general, however, it doesn't do many of the wonderful things that reading does.

Actually there are five important reasons why people should read. Except for the first one, they all help people to feel that they are more competent, and that's a feeling we all want to have.

1. People read because they want to enjoy themselves and escape for a while from the normal activities of everyday life.

2. They read to get help with a short-term goal. The goal may be something that interests them, but it doesn't have to be. It can be a goal such as fixing a leaky pipe or completing a school assignment.

3. They read to get help with a long-term goal, usually one that is more general. Perhaps, like you, they want to know how to help someone do better in school. Perhaps they want to know how to get along better with girls, or whether or not they should go to nursing school.

4. They read because they are concerned about important social issues or election candidates, and they want to know more in order to make up their minds.

5. They read because they are interested in some of the important ideas men have wondered about for centuries. In that case, they turn to our great classical writers.

Our less important, more temporary needs are at the top of the list. Our most important, most permanent needs are at the bottom of the list, and those are often the hardest ones for us to read about.

So Why Doesn't He Read?

If reading can help him do those important things, why doesn't your child read? One possibility is that he's just not competent at reading and doesn't get enough out of it to make it worth his while. If that's so, this chapter is not for you yet.

Earlier chapters of this book tell you what kinds of problems to look for and what to do about them. This chapter is concerned with the student who already has at least average skill in reading, but is reluctant to read.

One possible reason he doesn't read is that he doesn't see reading as an important part of the life of his family, or of other people significant to him. Of course, if he grew up in a house in which people normally turned to books to help solve their problems, the chances are he will slip into that habit as naturally as breathing or eating. Sometimes, however, a student doesn't acquire that habit even though the people around him use books a great deal. On the other hand, if you're trying to help your own child, and you are not a reader yourself, the child may say to himself: "You say it's important to read but you don't really believe it yourself. If you did, you would be reading too. If you can do without it, so can I." Your youngster is also unlikely to think of you as a reader if you limit yourself to newspapers and magazines. If you are trying to convince him it's desirable to read books without doing that kind of reading yourself, your argument is going to sound weak and insincere.

If you haven't been much of a reader, it's not too late. There is no good reason why reading shouldn't be enriching your life as well as your student's. Spend some time getting acquainted with your local library with your child. If your local library is small and has a poor collection, there is probably a larger, better collection in a neighboring town. Many libraries have record and tape collections that will interest your youngster too. In any case, let your youngster see you start to get interested in enjoyable fiction, how-to books, books about your work, and as many other kinds of reading as you can get interested in. Sometimes the fact that you have found out only recently how useful reading can be to you can be very dramatic and can make a big impression on your child.

Another reason your child may give for not reading is that he doesn't have the time. He probably honestly feels that he doesn't. There are many interesting activities that compete for his free time—socializing, sports, hobbies, watching TV. What he's saying is, "I feel that I get more pleasure or benefit from these other things than I do from reading." If he knew how enjoyable and helpful reading could be, he would make time for it, even if that meant having less time for other things. Time is like money. We never have enough of either to do all the things we want. As a result, we pick the things that are most important to us and spend our time and money on them. We give up doing the things we feel are less important. So don't try to argue him out of the "no time" position. If he feels that other things are more rewarding, you can't win by telling him that he doesn't feel that way. Instead of telling him something he "knows" isn't true, make reading more attractive and useful. Most of the rest of this chapter is designed to show you how to introduce him to reading that will "grab" him. If you can do that, the "no time" argument will fall away.

How to Get Them into Reading

How can we encourage people to read? Often it can't be done all at once, or quickly. Attitudes take years to develop, and frequently we can only chip away at them in bits and pieces.

A first step is to show your student that you respect reading and what it can do for you. There is no need to be heavy-handed. Don't call it to his attention every time you look at a book. If he sees you doing it, he'll get the idea, even if neither of you says anything about it. Of course, if a book really excites you, by all means talk about it to the family. Be alert to the interests of the other family members as you read. When you run across something you think they might find worthwhile, tell them about that too. Don't just aim those remarks at the person whose reading habits you want to change.

Respecting reading means other things too. It means that books are located in a convenient place in your home. It means that if your student does get into a book, you will see that he has a comfortable, quiet place to read. It means that you will interrupt him as little as possible to do other things. Frequent interruptions imply that reading is important all right, but somehow it's really more important that he do something else. It means that if we drive him to the library, we don't stand around on one foot and subtly put pressure on him to get out quickly because other things are making more important demands on our time. Obviously, our respect for reading is more evident in what we do than in what we say.

Using Family Activities to Encourage Reading

We can try to involve our youngsters in the kind of family problems for which reading is helpful. If the family is trying to decide what kind of car or appliance to buy, go to the library. The reference librarian can direct you to *Consumer Reports, Consumers' Research,* or other materials that describe how these products have been tested, and whether or not they are likely to meet your needs. After you buy the product, sit down with the people in the family who will be using it. Carefully read the guarantee and the manual that came with the product. These are good lifetime habits to build. As you know, some manuals are very hard to read and may require the assistance of others in the family. Why shouldn't our student see that everyone else is having a problem with it, not just him?

Reading helps to solve many problems that arise in the home. Repairs need to be made from time to time. For these, how-to books can be very helpful. If the family is trying to decide which TV program to watch or what movie to see, newspapers and magazines offer reviews that can help in making choices and can offer interesting ideas for discussion afterward. Is the family going on vacation to someplace new this year? If so, a trip to the library is likely to be well worth everyone's time and effort. Reading and talking about an area before you go to see it sharpens your appetite for the trip. It also tells you about many things to do and see that you might not otherwise discover. If your reluctant reader "overhears" two people in the family talking about something exciting in the vacation area that one of them has just read about, that can do no harm. Anytime anyone in the family reads something interesting or amusing, it's a good idea to share it at the dinner table. Many other sharing opportunities arise at home.

TV and Reading

Are you surprised that this book, which is devoted to developing better readers, has a section on using TV? After all, many people believe that TV has negative effects on children and their reading habits. I could easily fill many, many pages on those effects, but I'm going to mention just a few of them.

TV producers want to keep us from switching to another channel. To hold our attention they present interesting and enjoyable ideas rapidly and frequently. Therefore, these ideas must be easy to understand. Our attention is directed so quickly from one idea to the next that we can't really think very much about any of them.

One result is that we become passive receivers of information. Children are thus taught that learning is an easy and instantly enjoyable process. They are easily frustrated and lose interest if they have to work hard or get uncomfortable to learn, especially if there is no immediate pleasure in doing it.

The style of TV presentation introduces other problems. There is neither time nor encouragement for the viewer to differentiate between fact, opinion, and fantasy. Vocabulary development suffers because new and difficult words are introduced rarely, nor is there time to figure out the words we don't know.

Stories are presented in thirty- or sixty-minute time slots. To get them done within those rigid time limits, stories are often put together illogically, relying heavily on coincidence and with little regard for reality. This may encourage children to accept uncritically what is offered in the thinking and writing of themselves and others. TV hasn't taught them to look for logic or reality, or anything else that may be hard to understand.

However, I'm sure most of us wouldn't want to eliminate TV from our lives, in spite of the problems it causes. TV is here to stay. It's too convenient, too inexpensive a form of recreation, and too much a part of American life for us to tell our young people that they can't watch any of it. So perhaps we should try to use it in more sophisticated ways.

TV (and films) can do some things in education even better than books can. TV really reaches into the head of the viewer. It usually captures and holds his attention much more quickly than books do. When people talk to me while the TV set is on, I often find my eyes and mind repeatedly wandering over to the program, even when it's something I don't like. I have to turn off the set to pay attention to my friends.

TV and films are better than print for some kinds of learning jobs. If it's important to see and hear something to learn about it, TV and films should be used. They are very good at showing us what Niagara Falls looks and sounds like, or how different kinds of germs travel through water. In fact, they are good to use whenever sound, color, movement, and size are important in describing something.

TV and films have another great advantage too. Students find it very hard to learn about some things if they don't have previous experience with them. Let's take a simple example. If a student lives where getting enough water is never a problem, how can he hope to understand how the desert Arab lives? His clothes, work, food, transportation, his joy when he finds water and trees—these things are hard to teach through print because our pupil has nothing in his own experience to help him understand them. TV and film can show these things more quickly and meaningfully, and with more personal impact than print. They can thus quickly prepare students who otherwise lack the background to understand a topic.

In fact, TV stimulates reading for some children. Librarians report that a good TV adaptation of a children's classic sends many children to the library. They immediately borrow all the copies of that story they can find.

Try to be selective in the TV programs you watch yourself. Pick some good dramatic programs and some factual programs

that tell about the world around us. That's like leaving an open
jar of honey on the table. In time, the flies will come around to
sample it without a formal invitation. More important, your
youngster will feel it was his own idea, because nobody asked
him to come by. Given any luck at all, the TV's color, sound,
and movement will grab him from time to time without your
suggesting that he sit down and watch.

Some programs are well done and quite interesting. The science program "Nova" and Jacques Cousteau's programs on
nature are excellent. But don't worry about whether the programs you watch are good or uplifting. What you do with a
program is more important than its quality.

Good programs or poor ones, it's vital that you occasionally
break into the passivity that TV induces. To get all you and
your student can out of watching a program, and to use it as
a springboard into reading, turn the TV set off as soon as the
program ends. Why? Because if you leave the set on the next
program will draw your attention to other ideas. The best time
to discuss a program is when it's still fresh, before your mind
wanders off to something else. So turn it off, and start talking.
Feel free to praise, blame, or question what the program did.
Raise the questions that come naturally to you. Did the program suggest a question that it didn't answer? Did it mention
as a fact something that you doubt, or want to know more
about? Did it discuss the life and work of someone and make
you curious to know more? If so, fine. All of those reactions are
teasers. Nothing would be more natural than for you and your
student together to turn to a book in the house, or the library,
to answer the questions raised. It's important that the two of
you look for the information together, especially if the student
is normally reluctant to use books. You can help him over the
rough spots that occur in locating the information. If you're in
trouble, don't be afraid to ask a reference librarian for help.
Further, it gives acceptability and importance to a task if your
youngster sees it is something you do yourself.

In time, your student will learn a lot about locating the

information he wants in a library, because you have done it with him. For the same reason, he'll get used to the idea of reading to answer his own questions. In time he will need your help less and less to do these things.

Using TV properly does not include deciding that your child is watching something you don't like and insisting that he "turn off that nonsense and watch something uplifting instead." Few tactics are more likely to produce the opposite result. Instead, try to figure out what the youngster likes about the program. Perhaps you can suggest something else that fulfills the same need, next time.

The Youngster's Need to Read

TV is only one of the tools we can use to help move young people into reading. One of the most important allies you have in this battle is the person himself. The average youngster growing up has internal personal needs almost as strong as the need for food and water. Young people have a strong desire to learn to solve their own problems, and to have others see them as competent. Is there some connection between this drive for competence and the five important reasons why people read? You will remember that we listed those reasons as:

1. The need for relaxation and temporary escape from normal activity.

2. The need for help with a short-term goal.

3. The need for help with a long-term goal.

4. The need to learn about significant social issues.

5. The need to explore significant ideas.

In fact, these five reasons why people read are quite consistent with the desire to gain competence and respect. Reading can be a great help to young people in their drive for competence.

In any case, please remember that getting a reluctant youngster to read isn't easy. Don't be surprised if most of your suggestions aren't acted upon. If your student reads one of ten books you suggest, that's pretty good going. Do you always read the books your friends suggest? Don't be surprised (or hurt) if the youngster picks up one of your suggestions and doesn't finish it. The plain truth of the matter is that people take a long time getting to be the way they are. They make a lot of adjustments to enable themselves to be comfortable about not reading, and they don't change rapidly—they can't. So relax and be prepared to lose a few battles in the hope that you can eventually win the war. If you find yourself getting angry and resentful with the youngster because he doesn't take your suggestions, and interpret this as a rejection of yourself, you have two outs —watch out, and get out. There may be many reasons why the youngster rejects the suggestions you've made that have nothing to do with rejecting you. If you start to get hot under the collar, you are usually better off if you pull out of the situation.

So let's talk about getting your youngster into reading for the five reasons that other people read. The first one, reading for release from the pressure of everyday affairs, is a good one to start with. This kind of reading demands very little from the reader and gives him a lot of pleasure quickly. I suspect, too, that this kind of reading often meets the third reason that people have for reading—the desire to achieve some long-term goal. Thus Robert Lipsyte's *One Fat Summer* is the story of a fourteen-year-old who struggles with a weight problem. He finally overcomes it when he realizes that he is capable enough to take what life dishes out without having to overeat. This book is enjoyable because it's well-written and interesting. As such it fulfills the need to relax. However, it can be satisfying and important to any teen-ager who feels he has a problem to overcome, and is concerned about his worth as a person. He will probably respond sympathetically to the overweight boy's feelings. He may even learn something from the book about how to help himself feel better. Seeing how someone else overcame a problem almost always helps the reader feel better. The reader's problem doesn't have to have anything to do with being overweight. It's the feeling underneath that counts.

Certainly adults can't be expected to spend all their time reading young adults' books to find out which ones to recommend. Fortunately, that work has been done for you. Later in this chapter I'll tell you how you can inexpensively get a lot of information about books that are popular with young people.

The second need for reading that we listed concerned itself with short-term goals. These are often thought of as how-to matters. They concern things like cooking, making clothing, hobbies, household repairs, and specific school assignments. How-to books abound in every library and bookstore.

How do you find a book on some specific topic? At the library, look up your topic in the card catalog. Often each card briefly describes the contents and major thrust of the book. When you find the title of a book that you or your youngster thinks might be helpful, copy the number in the upper left-hand corner of the catalog card. Also copy the book's author and title. Do this for all of the books that might be helpful. Then go to the shelf or shelves indicated by the numbers you copied, and examine the books on your list. Use the table of contents and the index to see if each book contains the information you want. It takes a bit of patience but is well worth it.

If the books on the shelves don't have what you want, or if the card catalog doesn't list any books under your topic, don't panic. Is there another topic heading that might be helpful? For example, if there is nothing listed under "Cabinet Work," try looking up "Carpentry" or "Woodworking."

If you still can't find what you want, or want books that your library doesn't have, ask your reference librarian for help. She has other sources of information that may be helpful. Often she can direct you to a nearby library that has what you want. Or she can try to borrow the book from a more distant library. She may even be able to have your local library buy the book. Because buying the book or borrowing it from another library often takes a few weeks, it's a good idea not to wait until the last minute to find the books you need.

Your librarian will probably show you two excellent books to help you locate the information you want. One is the *Senior High School Library Catalogue,* edited by Estelle Fidel and Toby Ryan. The other is the *Junior High School Library Catalogue,* edited by Ilene Schechter and Gary Bogart. The junior high volume can be used for weaker senior high students, as well as for junior high students. Both books are used in the same way.

Turn to the index at the back of the book first. You can use it to look up a topic, an author's last name, or the title of a specific book. All of those are combined in that one alphabetical index. The index refers you to specific books, or to as few as five pages in some books, on a given topic. Fiction titles are marked "Fic." Nonfiction titles are marked with the Dewey decimal number that is used to locate the book on the shelf.

If the book is fiction, turn to the section of the catalog that is just before the index at the back of the book. Alphabetically under the author's last name, you will find an excellent brief description of the book's contents. You can use the description to tell if this book is likely to be appropriate or interesting. These descriptions are helpful if you want to tempt your youngster to read for information.

If the book is nonfiction, copy its Dewey decimal number and then look it up in the front of the *Senior* [or *Junior*] *High School Library Catalogue.* Here the Dewey decimal numbers are arranged in increasing numerical order. You will find a brief but accurate description of the contents of every book listed under each number. The descriptions help you to decide which book or books are likely to have the information you want.

If after all the trouble everyone has gone through to get the book, your youngster doesn't spend a lot of time reading it, don't despair. He may need to read only a few pages to solve his problem. The important thing is that your youngster gets the habit of using books to locate needed information. That's one of the ways that books can become a helpful and important part of his life.

Information dealing with the reader's long-term goals can be found in the same way. Of course, much of the time we don't search for that kind of material but find it by chance in something we are reading for another purpose, or when somebody recommends a book to us.

What about reading to fulfill the last two needs on our list— the need to learn about immediate social issues and the need to explore some of our most serious philosophic questions? These concern matters such as why man was put here on earth, or what is the real nature of good and evil. It's very important for people to think about these things. I certainly wouldn't want to convince anyone who reads or thinks about them that they shouldn't be doing so. On the other hand, it's unfortunately true that only a very small part of our population ever gets involved in these questions. Lester Asheim, for years the head of the graduate library school at the University of Chicago, estimates that less than 10 percent of us really become involved in reading on such serious matters, and he is undoubtedly right.

Why do we do so little reading to satisfy these needs? Nobody knows for sure, but I suspect two factors. One is that while these needs are extremely important in our lives, our students have many more immediate needs such as deciding how they will earn a living, getting along with people of the opposite sex, repairing something at home, or studying for a test. The truth is that the more immediate matters often crowd out the more important ones in our lives. So often we find ourselves neglecting to do things that are really important, simply because less important things are more pressing.

Another reason that we don't read or think about some of those important needs is that, quite simply, they often turn out to be extremely difficult to read about and understand. None of us likes the feeling that maybe we're not smart enough to understand something difficult to read, so we just don't make ourselves do it unless we have to. It isn't fair or sensible to demand that reluctant readers tackle the most difficult things to read, when most adults don't tackle them, and when it's difficult enough to get these youngsters to read easier and more enjoyable material. If anybody wants to read about serious social or philosophic problems they should certainly be encouraged to do so. If someone regularly reads to satisfy the first three needs of our list only, we should occasionally tempt him to read for the last two needs as well. But it just doesn't make sense to ask the reluctant reader to read material that he has the least chance of enjoying and understanding, until he has established the reading habit in easier material.

Finding Books Young People Like

To tempt your youngster to read for enjoyment, you should get to know which books are popular with young people in general and what each of these books is about. Again your local librarian can help. Libraries often have lists of books that are popular with "young adults." (Young adults are people between the ages of thirteen and eighteen, just the group that interests us.) There are other excellent sources of information. Most, if not all of them, are available at your local library.

1. The American Library Association's Order Department, Young Adult Services Division, 50 E. Huron St. Chicago, Ill. 60611, publishes a set of brochures yearly that cost ten cents each. They are prepared by a committee headed by Susan Tait. Each of them lists and briefly but interestingly describes about forty books of proven appeal and worth. There are a number of lists each year, including one called "Best Books for Young Adults," as well as other lists for this age group. Some local libraries reproduce these lists and offer them at no charge.

2. The American Library Association also publishes "Book Bait," edited by Elinor Walker. This was published in 1969, is 129 pages, and costs $2.50. Although this book list is older than many others, it does some things that are very helpful that the other book lists do not. Each book is discussed in one

to two pages. First there is a long, thorough summary of the book. Then "Book Bait" tells what kind of young person the book appeals to, and also tells what values it stresses. Then there is a brief discussion of how to interest youngsters in the book, which often includes the page numbers of particularly interesting or exciting parts of it. Finally, if the youngster likes the book, there is a short list of other popular books on the same or similar topics.

3. "High Interest-Easy Reading" is prepared by a committee headed by Marian White, for the National Council of Teachers of English. It costs ninety-five cents, was published in 1972, and has 140 pages of recommended titles, arranged by topic. The books selected met the following criteria: They had to be very interesting, easy to read, of good literary quality, attractive in appearance, and available for sale. This list does not include most of the classics, or books that are required reading in school. Each book is described in fifty to seventy-five words. This is a very good list. It was written to be read by children. It recommends books for junior and senior high youngsters. It is available from Citation Press, 50 W. 44 Street, New York, N.Y. 10036, and from the National Council of Teachers of English, 1111 Kenyon Road, Urbana, Ill. 61801.

4. "Books for You, A Booklist for Senior High Students" is prepared by a committee headed by Kenneth L. Donelson, of the National Council of Teachers of English. It costs $2.95, was published in 1976, and has 482 pages. Its titles are also arranged by topic under fiction and nonfiction, with a big section on films. The books and films have been selected on the basis of their appeal. Each title is discussed in from twenty to fifty words. This book is available from the same sources as "High Interest-Easy Reading."

Ask your local librarian for these books. She also has many other good lists of books for young people.

Bear a few things in mind if you are trying to interest an

unwilling reader. Many of these young people tell their teachers and librarians that they will only read "a thin book." So there is a better chance that a book you suggest will be read if it's thin, as well as interesting. Please understand, I am not happy with that recommendation. Whether a book is good has nothing to do with how many pages it has. But when you are trying to get someone to drop his reluctance to read, it's foolish to place unnecessary obstacles in his path. Once that reluctance begins to disappear, you can suggest a longer book from time to time, especially if you feel that it will be particularly interesting or valuable.

Everyone who deals with young people and their reading has agreed that paperbound books are much more popular than books in hardcover. That seems impossible to believe, because whether or not a book is good depends on its contents rather than its covers. In spite of that there is no denying it: They much prefer paperbound books. Paperbacks are less expensive, and their covers are usually more attractive. They are more convenient, too, and can be tucked easily into a pocket or a purse. There they are much less likely to cause comment by other youngsters who don't have much use for reading. Then too, paperbound books may be more popular because they don't look like school books. Whatever the reasons are, it can't be denied that paperbound books are much more acceptable to young people than hard-covered books are. If you are trying to get a reluctant youngster to read, a good paperback book is a better bet than that same book in hardcover.

Some magazines are quite popular with young people. A librarian in a high school that deals with middle-class children tells me that some of those children read only magazines. *Hot Rod, Sports Illustrated, People, Ebony, Esquire,* and *Car and Driver* are very popular. A subscription to one of these magazines can be an excellent gift.

You may be concerned that some of these magazines don't deal with topics that are "uplifting." That may also be a problem when you look at the description of some (but by no means all) of the books that young people like. It's interesting to notice that books about some of life's fairly serious problems are very popular. Solid youngsters who will grow up to live reasonably happy, satisfying lives are fascinated by books about young people who experience death in the family, or have an alcoholic or rejecting parent, have a drug problem, fall in love with somebody of another race, or are concerned about homosexuality. That's a pretty "heavy" set of topics. I can imagine some of you saying, "I'd rather my child didn't read at all, if those are the kinds of books he wants." Let's look at that problem.

Why should so many kids be fascinated by such behavior? A number of reasons combine to make this so. One is that adolescents are young people reaching into adulthood. They now want to read about more mature problems, maybe for the first time. They want to know and are very curious about what's out there in adult life—an area that has been forbidden to them up to now. And they are reassured when they read about other young people who solve problems more serious than their own.

Another reason is that adolescents are people (though that's hard to believe, sometimes) who are often flooded with strong feelings that clamor for release. Often these young people don't know how to let those feelings out in ways that we can accept. After all, they can't throw tantrums or do things younger people can do, and they haven't yet learned how adults blow off steam. An excellent safety valve for strong feelings is to become sympathetically involved in the intense problems of a character in a book. Then they can discharge lots of strong feeling. They do it quietly while they're reading, and it doesn't bother anybody else because there are no real people concerned whose feelings can be hurt.

Still another reason for reading about these topics exists. Our children are offered the possibility of behaving in many different ways. They see their parents' behavior, they see people doing things on TV and in films, and they see how many different kinds of people behave in school and in the neighborhood —all of which offer them many alternative behaviors to consider. Some of the ones we most hope they won't explore are very tempting. What better way is there to explore them than to read about them in a responsibly written book? A responsibly written book (and all the books on the lists I've recommended are just that) is one whose characters make mistakes and have weaknesses as well as strengths. You feel the author's respect for and sensitivity to human beings. When a book's characters experiment with behaviors they shouldn't experiment with, you share their pain when they are hurt. Would you rather your child experimented with these behaviors directly?

When a youngster has been thinking about experimenting with an activity that his parents disapprove of, he's much better off reading about it than doing it. An honestly written book will make the unpleasant consequences of that behavior painfully clear—and will do it with sympathetic involvement, without moralizing or lecturing. In other words, these books can often warn children about these behaviors far better than we can.

If He's Reading "Junk"

Some parents are concerned that their youngsters read nothing but "junk," material that is not well-written and has no lasting value. This situation calls for the parents to use sensitivity and tact.

Often we wait awhile to see if the youngster will change matters by himself. If he doesn't, we get more and more uncomfortable, until one day we find ourselves saying, "For heaven's sake, why don't you read something good for a change!" In responding to our annoyance, we're damaging our cause instead of helping it. By showing that our youngster's tastes and reading interests are unacceptable to us, we declare war. When we do that, we force the youngster to be our opponent and to defend what he has been doing. We don't permit him to give it up.

What we really want to do, whenever possible, is to support and accept our kids. We want them to think about the merits of the alternatives that we suggest, free of anger and defensiveness. That is a more realistic attitude when we feel that the youngster is restricting his reading to a steady diet of "junk."

Why does a youngster read "junk"? Because it's useful to him. He needs something the material provides. As adults, we tend to see only that the material is junk, and are unaware that it answers a need. Once we understand that need, we can hope that one day our student will learn to satisfy it with well-written material instead.

Tempting Him to Read Other Things

The way to accomplish that goal is not to deplore what the child reads, or to disregard his need to read it. First, find out what he finds useful or enjoyable in what he's reading now. You can do this in two ways. Ask him what he likes about the material he is reading. If you ask in a way that is free of judgment and criticism, you may find out. However, even when you get a reasonable answer, it may not be the correct one. People don't always know their own real reasons for doing things. So it's a good idea to read two or three of the things yourself that the youngster has recently enjoyed. See what common threads run through this material. This isn't a foolproof method, of course, but it's a way to start. When you think you know what kinds of writing interest your reader, look through some of the lists of recommended books I mentioned earlier in this chapter. Here is where the discussion of the contents and appeal of each book will be useful. Get some of the books that reflect the same appeal as the material your youngster is reading, and see if you can tempt him to read one of them.

There are several ways to tempt someone to read a book. You can talk about the book's central problem or conflict—but don't tell him how it comes out. Otherwise why should he read the book? Or, mention any aspect of the book that is of particular interest to your listener—sports, cars, romance, or what-have-you. If you've read some of the book and have enjoyed it yourself (and that isn't at all farfetched or surprising), talk about what you enjoyed. Just relax, and be sure that you are tempting rather than coercing or pressuring your youngster to read. After all, your side has a lot going for it. You're offering the youngster really good, enjoyable books that tell him a lot about what he wants to know. Sooner or later, you will probably succeed, so just relax and, in a low-key way, keep trying.

The One-Topic Reader

What if your student reads good books but only reads about one topic, such as baseball or horses? This really bothers some adults (but never the person who does the reading). How serious a problem is this? It's probably not a serious problem at all. In fact, it usually solves itself in a reasonable amount of time. Certainly this youngster *is* reading. Then too, adolescence is a time in which youngsters have intense interests, many of which do not last long. If your student only wants to read about horses for relaxation, let him. As soon as his hunger for this kind of information is satisfied, he'll read about something else that interests him. He'll give it up when he's ready. He won't be ready if you turn him away from reading about it before he's had his fill.

What about the youngster who reads a book that is too easy or too difficult for him? The key to whether or not this is a problem is consistency. The youngster who consistently takes books that are too easy or too hard for him is giving us a signal. If the books are too easy, he may be afraid to trust himself and his reading skills. If the books are too difficult, he may have some need to pretend that he can read difficult material, when in fact he can't. It might be helpful to talk over this problem with a sensitive teacher or guidance counselor.

If your student only occasionally reads material that is too easy or hard, that's not a source of concern. After all, when adults pick a book to read, its reading level is something they don't even consider. If the book fulfills the adult's purpose, he reads it. The only time the reading level is an issue is when the book is too difficult. Even so, many people can read books that are above their "grade level" if reading and understanding those books is important enough to them. Teachers often see a youngster successfully reading a book at a level that would ordinarily be too difficult for him. The key to his success is that he is intensely interested in the subject. This is also the single most important key to changing a reluctant reader into someone who enjoys books.

CHAPTER 9

"Where is the dessert?"

More than just being entertained by what we read, appreciation has two other aspects. One is an awareness that some authors can do quite remarkable, enjoyable things with words. The other is the realization that occasionally something we read offers insight into an issue or problem in our own lives —and we are permanently the richer for it. Our lives, from that point outward, are different because of what we've read.

Why a Chapter on Appreciation?

It may seem strange to include a chapter on appreciation in a book devoted to helping students to learn to read for information more effectively. But after all, reading is not something people do only to satisfy the requests and needs of others— which is how I suspect many of our young people see it. The more they see it that way, and the more difficulty they have in fulfilling the school's requirements, the more important I think it is for them to be exposed to the pleasures and benefits that reading can bring. Concentrating only on the "business" end of reading is a lot like saying, "As you eat this steak, I want you to concentrate only on the nutrition it gives you. Disregard the wonderful flavor and softness of it altogether." Wouldn't that be silly!

Share What You Enjoy

If a school subject particularly appeals to you, why hide that? You can't tell other people that they must find pleasure in it because you do. However, if you show that this material gives you pleasure, that may be a brand-new idea for your student. In time, some of it may "rub off" on him.

I particularly remember my high school plane geometry teacher in this regard. He did the demonstrations that proved the various theorems with such lip-smacking relish that I began to wonder what he found so pleasurable. I think that he must have liked the neatness, the precision, the efficiency of the proofs. Once you accepted the basic assumptions of plane geometry, each theorem seemed to say: "You can use me to solve other problems—but first you must establish logically that what I state is valid. Can you do that?" With that problem stated, each succeeding step in the proof flowed tightly and logically from what came before —and flowed just as tightly and logically into what came next. There was nothing that was wasted or unnecessary in the proof, just as there was nothing in it which was indefinite, or uncertain. And the explanation always ended at the point at which it had accomplished just what it had been intended to do. These explanations were logically tight, efficient, and incontrovertible. Wasn't it great to feel that you had solved a problem with neatness and certainty, and didn't have to be concerned with any "buts" or "maybes"? Wouldn't it be nice if the other problems in our lives could be solved so neatly and quickly, and with never a need to wonder if we had done the right thing for the right reasons?

To tell the truth, I don't know if these were the reasons that my teacher liked those geometry proofs so much—and that really isn't important. The point is that his showing me that he enjoyed the material stimulated my own appreciation of it— something I probably would not have developed if not for his leadership by example.

A Sample Appreciation Lesson

Let's take a short passage and see what can be done to help us, the readers of this book, to appreciate it. Then we'll review the principles that were used so that you can use them in an occasional appreciation session.

Here is a passage from *Hard Times* by Charles Dickens, one of the great masters of the English language. It's a short passage. After you read it once, jot down your first reactions to it. My object is to show you how a few simple things can help you to enjoy what is at first a perplexing passage.

> "Bitzer," said Thomas Gradgrind, "your definition of a horse." "Quadruped. Gramnivorous. Forty teeth, namely twenty-four grinders, four eye-teeth, and twelve incisive. Sheds coat in the Spring; in marshy countries sheds hoofs too. Hoofs hard, but requiring to be shod with iron. Age known by marks in mouth." Thus (and much more) Bitzer. "Now girl number twenty," said Gradgrind, "you know what a horse is."

Now that you've read it once, please jot down your first reactions. Don't worry if you're uncomfortable about the passage. It should be quite difficult to understand, much less appreciate, at this point.

Now please go back and reread the passage a few times, slowly. You will probably get more out of it.

I usually ask my students to reread a passage a few times too. I then ask them to share with the rest of the class whatever reactions they have. When you work with your student, expect his reactions to be given slowly, and cautiously, especially at the beginning.

Here are some typical student reactions, together with my responses:

JEAN: I thought it was funny that he called her "girl number twenty."

TEACHER: Yes—and what did he call the male student?

MARY: Mr. Gradgrind called him by name, "Bitzer."

TEACHER: Yes. What does that suggest about Mr. Gradgrind's attitude toward males and females?

MARY: He's saying only the boys are worth remembering. It's too much trouble to remember the girls' names, so he just gives them numbers. He makes the girls less important, less human.

TEACHER: That's very good. Did anybody else get any other feelings they would like to share with us?

BILL: I don't think "girl number twenty" really knew what a horse was at all, from this definition.

TEACHER: That's a good point. Tell us why.

BILL: I don't know. It's all bits and pieces. But none of it really gives you a feeling of what a horse is really like.

TEACHER: Ah, but what is Mr. Gradgrind's reaction to the definition?

BILL: He likes it; there's no question about that.

TEACHER: So what does this tell us about Mr. Gradgrind's feelings about how to educate people?

BILL: He seems to feel that education is getting people to memorize a lot of little facts.

TEACHER: Is he interested at all in getting them to draw conclusions from those facts, in getting them to see where those groups of facts lead, or in asking students to tell how they feel about these facts?

BILL: No, he just wants people to memorize what he tells them to, and recite it on demand.

TEACHER: How do you think Dickens felt about this kind of education?

JOAN: He didn't like it.

TEACHER: What makes you say that?

JOAN: After Bitzer gives his definition, Gradgrind feels that the girl should know what a horse is, and it's obvious that the definition hasn't told her at all.

TEACHER: That's right. Any other reaction to this passage?

TOM: What does *gramnivorous* mean?

TEACHER: Good! I'm surprised nobody has asked up to now. I didn't know either, and I didn't find it until I looked in three or four dictionaries. *Carnivorous* means "meat-eating," *herbivorous* means "plant-eating," and *gramnivorous* means "grain-eating." I was delighted when it wasn't in the first three dictionaries I looked at. I thought Dickens was trying to show that Gradgrind would even accept nonsense words if they sounded impressive, rather than admitting that he didn't know something. But *gramnivorous* turned out to be a real word. Any other reactions to the passage? No? Let me read it to you the way I think Dickens felt it should sound. [Teacher reads it to the class, while standing stiffly at attention. It is read loudly, rapidly, without expression and with clipped and forceful articulation, except for the last sentence. This, in contrast, is read slowly and with much expression.] Now, do you get a different feeling about what Dickens is trying to say?

CAROL: It sounded almost military, as though you were barking orders.

TEACHER: Warm and personal?

CAROL: No, cold and impersonal.

TEACHER: Well, that's consistent with depersonalizing the girls by giving them numbers instead of calling them by name, isn't it? But I want to call your attention to something else. Have you noticed that almost none of the passage's sentences are complete except for the last one? Either they lack a subject or a verb. None is complete, except for the last one. Do you think that a writer like Dickens didn't even know how to construct a sentence? Or did he hope to achieve some purpose?

JOEL: Maybe he meant to show how depersonalized the school was, with people talking more like machines than like human beings.

TEACHER: That's very likely, and I think he had another reason too. Why would a writer use incomplete sentences steadily, and then suddenly switch to a complete one?

HELEN: As a means of calling attention to the last sentence by making it so different?

TEACHER: Right—contrast is often used when the author wants you to be sure to notice something. So what did Dickens especially want you to notice?

HELEN: That Gradgrind actually felt that she really knew what a horse was because she heard that definition, which was downright silly.

TEACHER: Fine. Now let's talk about the names Dickens used. We've already talked about the significance of the "girl number twenty." What about the names "Bitzer" and "Gradgrind"? After all, Dickens had complete freedom—he could have chosen any names he wanted to. Was he trying to tell us something when he chose these names?

WILLIAM: Well, Bitzer only spits out bits and pieces of information.

TEACHER: That's good. Anything else?

MARCELLA: Maybe there's a connection between Bitzer and the bit that is in the horse's mouth.

TEACHER: Maybe. Can anybody else help?

GEORGE: Gradgrind just grinds out graduates. Or maybe he just grinds down the graduates of other schools who have come to him, with his emphasis on nothing but details.

TEACHER: So Dickens uses names to tell you something about the people who bear them. Let me ask you something else. About when was this passage written?

ELLY: In the 1850s.

TEACHER: And how do you suppose girl number twenty had gotten to school that day?

ELLY: On a horse!

TEACHER: Quite likely she was either on a horse or in a vehicle pulled by one. Or else, if she walked to school, she had to avoid evidence that horses had been in the neighborhood recently! What does this tell you about Gradgrind and his view of education?

ELLY: He didn't even see that he was teaching kids things they already knew.

TEACHER: So let's see. Dickens has told us not only what education was like in the nineteenth-century classroom in England, he has also told us a lot about what Mr. Gradgrind himself is like. Further, Dickens has made his opinions about Gradgrind and the kind of education he supported quite clear to us. (Would you like to be in a class taught by Mr. Gradgrind?)

If we were to list all the ideas and opinions Dickens gave us in this passage, we would probably need several hundred words to do it. Do you know how many words Dickens used to convey the same ideas? Just sixty-nine! Now I think we have a clearer idea of what we mean when we talk about "evocative writing!"

How to Make an Appreciation Lesson Work

Go back to the reactions you jotted down after your first reading of the Dickens passage. If you feel differently about it now, we helped you to appreciate it. What did we do (and what can you do, in other lessons) to promote appreciation?

1. Select something that discusses a topic that your reader has some experience with and can relate to.

2. Be sure that you get a kick out of what you select. It's a lot easier to interest somebody in something that you yourself really like.

3. Before you give the passage to the student, go over it yourself a few times when you're in a relaxed mood. Talk about it to friends who might enjoy it. In other words, get as many interesting and enjoyable reactions to the passage as you can.

4. Introduce the topic, so that your student feels more comfortable because he knows a little about what he's getting into. I *did not* do that in presenting the Dickens material. It didn't help you at all to come to it "cold," did it?

5. Ask the student to read it to himself a few times to let the newness wear off. This also lets the reader "feel" the material better.

6. Do an oral, dramatic reading of the passage, in which your expression, pace, and volume carry the feelings that the words produce in you. This will help produce them in your listener too.

7. Ask the reader to tell what feelings the material produced in him. This permits each of you to feel things about the passage that might not otherwise have occurred to you.

8. When the student's reactions are not consistent with the material or don't enhance appreciation of it, acknowledge the response politely, but whenever possible don't make any further comment on it. (Note how I dealt with Marcella's remark.) Sometimes it's difficult to get a student to tell you about his reactions. If you are negative or critical, you will probably discourage him from sharing his other reactions with you.

9. When it's clear that the student won't produce all the reactions that you want him to, feel free to express those reactions yourself.

10. By all means discuss style during the appreciation period. We did—we talked about Dicken's use of names, choice of sentence structures, and the number of words he used to convey his ideas. However, we should only analyze those

elements of style that help us get interesting new insights into the material, or help us to understand what an unusual piece of writing it is. One of my high school English teachers came close but missed the boat when he taught us about Shakespeare's sonnets. He made us analyze them to show both the rhythm and the rhyme patterns that Shakespeare used. It seems to me now that we spent hours doing that. Then, unfortunately, he just dropped the subject. But suppose he had gone on to point out that Shakespeare not only produced ideas that people still regard as beautiful and enjoyable four hundred years later, but did this in spite of the fact that he had imposed almost impossible restrictions on himself, and then met them. He wrote beautiful, original ideas but in words that had to conform to arbitrary and relatively rigid patterns of rhythm and rhyme. Do *you* think *you* could do that? But when we only analyzed the poetry and didn't use that analysis to help us understand how remarkable the poems were, we regarded the analysis only as a tiresome bore.

11. Sometimes it's important to point out the period in history, or the part of the world in which the material was written. We can only feel the full depth of Dickens's contempt for the waste and stupidity of memorizing a disjointed, piecemeal definition of a horse when we realize that in those days everybody in the class already knew what a horse was.

12. Although I didn't do it here, it often helps to review pertinent information about the life of the author. For instance, Dickens's father was employed, but was unable to handle financial affairs well. In 1822, the family moved to London, when Dickens was ten years old. Their finances went downhill rapidly. Young Charles was withdrawn from school and lived in poverty with his family. In 1824 Dickens's father was arrested and sent to debtors' prison. Charles, at age twelve, had to support himself and found a job pasting labels on bottles for six shillings a week. Although his father re-

ceived a legacy and was released from prison in May, 1824, Charles had been plunged into despair so deep that even later in life he could never bring himself to talk about these events. These experiences and their impact appear again and again in his writings.

As you can see, an appreciation lesson can involve some preparation and thought for the teacher. But appreciation is important and can be richly rewarding.

Sometimes in a discussion a student will question whether a given interpretation was actually what the author intended. Often we can't be sure. Even if the idea is consistent with the author's values, we may still not know if he wanted us to draw this conclusion, unless he specifically tells us elsewhere that he did. But this is not an important question. The point is that whatever was in the author's mind, something interesting and valuable happened in ours, and we are the richer for it.

Appreciating Other Material

Sometimes your student finds that doing required reading is a very painful task, but often it need not be. In almost any good book you will find (and can emphasize) issues that are important to *your* reader. How do you know which issues they are? That's easy. First make a list of the developmental problems and concerns that your student has. Getting along with people of both sexes, learning to decide issues for himself instead of having others do it, choosing what his life's work will be, and learning to adjust to a world in which many things are not what he has been told they are, are fairly common problems for teen-agers. You may know other issues that concern him. Now skim the assigned book yourself. Note how the people in the book struggle with the same kinds of problems. Your student and the people in the book don't need to be the same age, social class, or culture. They will be dealing with similar problems. These and the feelings that the reader and the author's characters share can be used to interest your pupil in the book and make it useful to him. The book's other issues can usually receive less attention, although the reader must be aware of the plot itself. If the student enjoys the book, he may return to it years later. At this point he may have other personal issues of concern to himself, and may find that the book offers additional feelings and insights. The point is that a worthwhile book is like a diamond. As we view it from different angles, its different facets can show us different approaches, and different kinds of light. It seems silly not to use the accumulated wisdom of our greatest minds when it is available to us in this way.

CHAPTER 10

"I just remembered— I have a report due on Monday!"

(For maximum effect, the above line should be spoken on Sunday evening.)

The student I quote in the chapter title had a problem all right—in fact, he had more than one. However, the "I-don't-get-to-work-until-it's-too-late" problem usually occurs simply because the student is intimidated by a task that he doesn't know how to do.

That's why this chapter was written. Step by step it tells how a student can do a paper—everything from picking a topic at the beginning, through all the other steps, to proofreading the paper at the end.

Selecting a Topic

The student must first decide what subject to write about. If the teacher assigns a specific topic, that problem is solved. But quite often the teacher only suggests a general area, and the student picks his own topic within that area. That's often the source of a number of difficulties.

Chief among these is the tendency to do too much too soon. Some students are so anxious to start the task (and get it over with) that they plunge in too quickly. They start to read and take notes immediately—which is bad. Why take notes before the topic has been selected? It's quite likely that many of these notes will not be useful, since they have not been gathered with a specific topic in mind.

Another "too much, too soon" problem arises when the student, again under his own pressure to be finished, picks the topic of his report too quickly. Too often, the only reason for picking that topic is that it is there. The topic is selected in order to relieve the discomfort of not having one, and to let the student get into the task. That's understandable, but why should the student pick a topic before he has considered the field and knows what other topics are available? Why should he pick the first or second topic he encounters, when others may be more interesting or valuable to him? *Why should he pick a topic before he knows how much reference material is available on it?*

The first step in picking the right topic is a quick overview of the field. For this purpose, encyclopedia articles are excellent —much better than whole books devoted to the general area or some part of it. Not only are those articles relatively brief, but they offer three other advantages. They are generally written by authorities in that field. They open many possibilities for the student to select a topic for his paper because, as overviews do, they tell him which specific subjects are included under the general area. Lastly, they provide references—books and articles he can read that will provide more information when he needs it.

Of course, if the general subject is something quite current, the student may not be able to find an encyclopedia article on it. Encyclopedia articles cover past history rather than current affairs. He should try the *Reader's Guide to Periodical Literature* and *The New York Times Index* in that case. There are a number of indexes to publications in various technical areas. Chapter II of James M. MacCrimmon's book, *Writing with a Purpose,* gives a fairly complete list of useful reference works. One reference librarian became my friend forever when she introduced me to books called "explicators." These list contemporary authors' works by category—plays, novels, short stories, etc. Each of the author's titles is listed, and below it is given a list of its published critical reviews, with enough information to tell you how to locate each one. Explicators are a real boon if you have to do a paper for an English class.

Libraries contain many good general-purpose encyclopedias such as *Compton's,* the *Book of Knowledge,* and the *World Book.* If these don't contain the overview the student needs, he should tell his problem to a good reference librarian and ask her for help. She will direct him to specialized encyclopedias on science, history, literature, and many other sources that most people don't know exist.

But whether the overview comes from an encyclopedia or some other source, it's important that the student read it in a relaxed, receptive frame of mind. He should be constantly asking, "What aspect of this area sounds as though it would make an interesting paper?" For example, if the general area is the Spanish-American War, an overview might suggest the following topics:

1. The causes of the war

2. Its military aspects

3. The results of the war, short-term and long-term

4. Changes in the world position of Spain and the United States as a result of the war

5. The role of the press in causing the United States to enter the war

Although the specific topic of the paper should not be rushed into, it should be chosen reasonably quickly. A student who has four weeks to do a paper can't afford to spend three and a half weeks looking for a topic. Possibly 10 percent of the four weeks would be a reasonable time to devote to the hunt for a topic.

Locating the Needed Information

Now that a topic has been selected, the reading can be much more purposeful and selective. To find sources, the student should look at the bibliographies at the end of the encyclopedia (or other overview) articles, at the end of the appropriate chapter in his history text, and in the school and local library catalogs.

A library catalog lists each book in the library in three different places: once according to the first initial of the author's last name; once according to the first initial of the first word in the title, usually excluding such words as *The, A,* or *An;* and once under the book's general topic or subject. Librarians don't always have the time to enter all three cards, so if a reference is important, the student should look for it in all three categories. The general topic (i.e., Spanish-American War) will refer him to all the books on the subject that are available at his library, many of which he might not otherwise be aware of. The book title and the material on the catalog card will often describe the contents of the book, enabling the student to decide whether or not this particular work is likely to be helpful. If such information is not otherwise available, the student can survey the content of appropriate parts of the book, using the technique described in this book's Chapter 7, which deals with speed-reading.

Planning and foresight are very important here. The student who thinks carefully about what he does, and also considers the advice of others who have gone that way before him, can save himself a lot of time and unnecessary work.

Some of the work done in preparing a paper will not be used in the final product. Of course, the student would prefer not to waste time doing things that don't find a place in the paper, but some effort of this kind is inevitable. Let's differentiate, however, between things that are necessary and helpful in doing the paper even though they don't appear in it, and things that involve unnecessary work, done primarily because the student didn't know better, or wasn't careful enough.

In the former category, the student read a few overview articles. Most of the material read will not appear in the paper. Was reading them unnecessary? No—he needed to read those overviews to help him decide what the possibilities were, and which topic he would finally select. However, suppose that in reading other references he takes notes that don't identify the page number or the author and title of the book from which that information came. And suppose further that on reading these notes two weeks later, he is not quite sure of what he meant. Now he has to interrupt what he's doing, go back to the library, find the book, and possibly read or at least skim or scan several pages in order to find the information. All of this was unnecessary, a wasteful repetition of effort.

Once the student has a topic, he needs three other things: (1) a bibliography or list of sources of information for his paper; (2) a body of information about the topic he's chosen; and (3) an outline or tentative plan of the subtopics he plans to discuss in his paper.

Constructing a Bibliography

The bibliography serves two different purposes. It starts out as a list of books and articles that may contain useful information for the paper. Each book or article to be looked up should be listed on a separate three-by-five-inch index card. The card should contain the author's full name, with the last name first, the title of the book, the name of the publisher, the city and year of publication. For a magazine article, the student should write the author's full name (last name first again), the title of the article in quotes, the name of the magazine, its date, its issue and folio numbers as given on the magazine cover, and the page numbers of the article. (If the teacher wants this information in the final bibliography in some other order, he will tell the student, and his request should be respected.) I am including a sample library catalog card below. The student's reference card need include only the information on the first three lines, and possibly the Library of Congress call number at the bottom.

913. Glueck, Nelson, 1900–
3945   Rivers in the desert; a history of the Negev.
              New York, Farrar, Straus and Cudahy 1959
              302 p. illus. 24 cm.
                1. Negev-Antiq. I. Title
              DS 110 N4G5   913.3945   59–5609
              Library of Congress 25   59–5609

The title card is exactly the same, but the words "Rivers in the desert" are typed above the author's name. The subject card is also exactly as the card above, except then the words "NEGEV-ANTIQUITIES" are typed in above the author's name.

Libraries arrange their nonfiction books in one of two ways. One of these is the Dewey decimal system, and the other is the Library of Congress system. The number 913.3945 that appears in the upper-left-hand corner of the card tells us where to locate this book in a library organized according to the Dewey decimal system. The author's name is given, and then the book's title. The third line from the bottom shows where other catalog cards describing this book are filed. The next to last line gives the Library of Congress system's call number, and then the Dewey decimal system number for this book. The rest of the information given on the card is either self-evident or unimportant for our purposes.

As the student reads each reference, he should mark the bibliography card "useful" or "not useful," but he should not throw the card away if the book has not been useful. If the information-gathering process lasts for a while, he will forget whether or not he has seen some of the books. Looking back at his alphabetized bibliography file can keep him from checking the same book twice.

Some readers may wonder why the student is advised to use one title to an index card, or why he should go to the expense of using index cards at all. Why can't he list all the references on one or more sheets of paper?

Once he writes the paper, the answer will be clear. Index cards can be arranged alphabetically. It's much more convenient to alphabetize a final bibliography on index cards than it is to do it from one or two sheets of paper which list the references in the order in which the student first encountered them. Also, in the later stages of gathering information, when he runs across additional references, it will be much easier for him to tell whether or not he already has made a note of a given reference if he can look it up alphabetically.

As the student starts to read the references, he should look for information pertinent to his paper. At this point, as when he first read the overviews, he is looking for information, plus some help in planning. He knows the specific topic of his paper, but probably needs to know what subtopics belong in the discussion and in which order they should be presented. Even if the student has a fairly good idea of how to organize his paper at the beginning of his search of the references, he should be flexible. If an area comes along that he didn't know existed, and it would clearly strengthen his paper, he should revise his original plan and put it in.

What if Necessary Information Can't Be Found?

Sometimes the student needs information for his paper, but he can't find it, or the local library doesn't have it. This is a very common problem. Finding reference information has become very difficult in the last twenty years. The number of reference works and sources has proliferated to such a degree that people like us have little chance of finding what we want unassisted. When I get stuck, I try to pick the most knowledgeable-looking, professionally trained reference librarian I can find, and put my problem to her. She is almost invariably happy to be asked for help and, within minutes, puts information into my hands that I didn't even know existed and would have spent frustration-filled hours discovering on my own. Of course, I never ask a reference librarian for help without having looked up the topic in the library's card catalog, and having seen what is available on the open shelves. If I find that my library has very few of the references I have listed, I return to my librarian friend and explain my problem.

There are several ways in which she may be able to get the materials the student needs, at little or no cost. She can find out which local libraries have these books on hand. If the library is too far away to visit, it may be tied in to an interlibrary loan system. This means that Library A lends material to Library B (the students' hometown library). Library A will often Xerox brief articles and mail them to Library B if requested. There are other ways in which the librarian can get materials that are not usually available where she works.

All of this underscores two necessities. The student should look for his reference materials as early as he can. If his classmates get to the library first and borrow the books he needs, they won't be available when he wants them. And if the materials he needs must be borrowed from another library, that can take a few days to a few weeks. Further, since promising-looking reference materials sometimes contain little or nothing that proves useful, the student should ask for more reference materials rather than less. When he's pressed for time, it may be disastrous for him to pin his hopes on only one or two books, which may turn out to be useless, or close to it, when they finally arrive.

The Importance of Index Cards

The student should use index cards not only for the bibliography, but to make an outline, and to record the information that will be used in the paper. (He should use cards of different colors for these tasks, so that he can tell them apart quickly.) Again, I urge him not to invent the wheel all over again. By that I mean that others have struggled with this problem before and have painfully learned that what looks like the most efficient way to do things at first, later turns out to be quite the opposite. As a case in point, it seems inefficient and expensive to record information on index cards, writing only one small point per card. However, these cards can be rearranged in any order as often as necessary. Most people rearrange them several times as their outline or writing plan takes shape.

They also rearrange the outline. When they gather information, they usually find material that belongs in the paper but doesn't appear in the outline, so the outline must be revised.

It's easy for the student to make these revisions by adding, pulling out, or rearranging index cards. By contrast, an outline that has been written on a sheet of paper is much more permanently fixed. It's hard to change even small pieces of it, so the student has to write the whole thing over almost every time he changes it. Index cards save a lot of wear and tear on the nerves.

To record the data collected for the report, the student should write on the upper-right-hand corner of each index card the subtopic this information should be included under —in pencil, because he can change his mind several times about which subtopic it should go under. Each card should also tell the source from which its information came. This need be no more than the author's last name, so long as there's a complete bibliography card for the book elsewhere. If the student has two or more references by the same author, he should include the date of publication of this particular source. He should also note the number of the page or pages that yielded this information. The page number is usually cited in the final paper if a direct quote is given. Even if he is not using the quote, should he wish to clarify in his own mind what he wrote on the card, the page number will enable him to get to the right page in the text quickly to check it. I can't tell how many times I have been happy I wrote that page number down, and it's so little trouble to do as the student takes notes.

After the student has taken notes from several sources, and has seen what a number of authors say about his topic, he is ready to write a final outline. Once he has written it, he should wait a day or so, then look at it and ask himself the following questions about it:

1. Is this outline an appropriate, direct response to the task I set myself in writing on my topic?

2. Do the subtopics in my outline flow tightly and logically from one to the next?

3. Have I left out any major areas—or have I included areas
   that don't belong in this paper? If so, correct these problems
   at once.

He should then categorize his information cards, subtopic by
subtopic, and put the cards in each subtopic in logical order.
The batches of subtopic cards are arranged in the order suggested by his outline. Next he reads through the cards. As he
finishes each subtopic, he asks himself, Is there enough information here? If there is not, he makes up a specific assignment
sheet. On it, he notes what gaps need to be filled, and next to
each, he indicates which subtopic this information will join.
Then he goes out to find the required information, notes it on
index cards as before, and arranges the new index cards in the
correct order under the appropriate subtopics.

The First Draft

Now the student can begin to think about writing the paper.
Two pieces of general advice are appropriate. He should assume that the first copy is a rough draft rather than the final
copy. A working copy can be changed here and there quite
comfortably, since its crossed out words and sentences will not
appear in the finished copy. Usually the working copy requires
many small changes.

The basic plan or outline may need change, as the paper
develops. Here the writer may decide that it would have been
better to leave out something that was put in. There he may
decide to add a sentence or a paragraph to make the connection
between two ideas smoother, or clearer. Or, as the writing is
based on notes from three-by-five cards, he may write a lot of
material and then find information that should have been included earlier. This is a very common problem.

There is another important reason to write a rough copy first.
Often, the student wants to express an idea but finds it difficult
to put into words. He should write the thought down, no matter
how poorly stated it seems. Once it's written (preferably dou-

ble-spaced at least), it's there to revise and polish a little at a time, until the writer is content with it. If it isn't put on paper until the sentence is acceptable, it will be much more difficult to revise. The writer must then divide his energy between remembering what the sentence says, deciding which parts don't look or sound right, and figuring out how to state those parts differently. By writing his first thoughts down, even though he knows that they will not be expressed properly, the writer can do these jobs one at a time. Therefore, they can be done more rapidly, easily, and effectively. Since this process involves crossing out words and phrases and rewriting them until a satisfactory sentence appears, it makes the content of the paper better while making its appearance worse. This is yet another reason to write a rough first copy.

Be Sure to Outline First

In no instance should the student start to write the first draft unless he is working from a satisfactory outline—although the temptation to do so is often enormous. Writing without an outline is a terribly wasteful procedure. Unless he writes according to a plan, he will later find it necessary to fit new material into nonexistent spaces between paragraphs that were written previously. Then the older paragraphs will need to be rewritten so that the new material fits smoothly between them. In other instances ideas are unintentionally repeated because of the lack of planning. This rewriting, and the delay and annoyance caused by having to do it, can be eliminated by outlining first and writing afterward.

Term papers should be written in formal style. The kind of language a youngster uses when talking with his friends is fine in that setting, but does not belong in a paper. Teachers find that this is a common fault in the papers they read.

The Final Copy

The appearance of the final copy is important. A paper that has many deletions, or looks as though it might have been used as a napkin or bed-sheet, speaks for its writer, and seems to be saying, "I didn't get this done in time to make a neat copy." Or, "I'm a sloppy or careless person." Or, "I just don't think the project you assigned was worth doing neatly." None of these impressions is likely to be looked on with favor by the person grading the paper.

Checking the Paper

It's a good idea to avoid as many deletions as possible in the final paper. If the paper is typed, correction fluids are available that cover the errors and enable the typist to type over them. Errors on handwritten papers cannot usually be completely hidden. Neatly draw a line through the words to be deleted and go on. If a page has too much deleted material in it, do it over. The student should write on only one side of each sheet. It's less work to copy one page over than two.

If the rough copy is proofread carefully, the final copy will need fewer corrections. Here are some common errors.

Does the paper have an introduction, a body, and a conclusion? If so, each of these areas must meet certain requirements.

An introduction should prepare the reader for what is to come. It should raise questions, stimulate curiosity, and generally convince the reader that he wants to read the rest of the paper. But the introduction shouldn't answer the questions it raises, no matter how briefly. If they are answered so soon, why would anyone bother to read the rest of the paper? Sometimes it's possible to discuss the significance of the topic, especially if the paper deals with a technical or historical subject. In any case, when the reader finishes the introduction, he should be able to say to himself, "I clearly and accurately know what the writer's purpose was in doing this paper."

In the body of the paper is there a smooth, logical flow from the introduction through each of the major subtopics, down to the conclusion? Are there enough details offered to satisfy the purpose of each subtopic? Are the details relevant, or are some repetitious or otherwise inappropriate? Teachers generally agree that a major problem in report writing is that students copy information indiscriminately out of reference sources—because it is vaguely connected to the topic, "because it is there," or because the student wants to make the paper longer. Extraneous material should be cut mercilessly. Its presence does more harm than good.

The concluding paragraphs should reflect the student's original purpose in writing the paper. However, the conclusion should not simply repeat the material in the introduction. It can briefly recapitulate the paper's main points and draw conclusions. Or it can answer the questions raised in the introduction. Or it can briefly discuss the subsequent impact of the events covered in the paper. There should be a sense of the writer's having accomplished what he set out to do, so that as a result the paper has come to a natural end.

Throughout his review of the paper, the student should be concerned about paragraph structure. Does the paper set forth each new significant idea in its own paragraph? Two or more significant ideas don't belong in the same paragraph. If you fail to get this idea across to your student quickly, don't pursue the point too long. It is better left to the professional teacher if it offers too much difficulty.

Proofreading is important. Ideally, a really good paper has excellent organization and content, and has been proofread carefully. Whether it's otherwise excellent, average, or poor, if it has been proofread poorly, the grade assigned to it will almost invariably be lower. A paper that has poor content, weak organization, and ineffective proofreading has little chance of passing.

Few kinds of errors are as obvious to the reader as spelling errors. Whoever does the proofreading should use a good dictionary to check the spelling of words that look questionable. Here are some spelling rules. Although these rules have exceptions, their use will help to eliminate many spelling errors.

1. The letters *g* and *c* are said to be hard (u*g*ly, ba*c*teria) or soft (ra*g*e, spa*c*e). They have the soft sound when they are followed by *i, e,* or *y.* Otherwise they have the hard sound. Look at the first letter of any suffix that you add to a word that ends with either sound of the letters *c* or *g,* and be careful not to change the sound. For example, you have to double the *g* to keep it hard when you go from *big* to *biggest.* You have to drop a final *e* after a soft *c* or *g* if the suffix you add starts with *i, e,* or *y.* Thus we go from *race* to *racing,* from *cage* to *cagy.* All you have to remember is to keep the same *g* or *c* sound as the word had before, and that *i, e,* and *y* make those sounds soft.

2. Plural forms are often misspelled. If a word ends in *f* or *fe,* change those letters to *ves* in the plural (li*fe,* li*ves*).

   Compound words (brother-in-law) get the *s* added to the most important word of the group (brother*s*-in-law), unless the compound ends in *ful* (spoonful*s*).

3. If words that have only one sounded vowel end with a vowel and a consonant in that order (c*ap*), the consonant is doubled before adding a suffix that starts with a vowel (ca*pp*e*d*).

4. If words end in *ie,* those letters are changed to *y* before adding *ing* (t*ie,* t*y*ing).

5. If words end in a consonant and a *y* in that order *(lazy),* the *y* is changed to an *i* before adding any suffix (laz*i*ness). To add an *s* to such a word (melod*y*) change the *y* to *ies* (melod*ies*).

6. Should it be *ie* or *ei?* The old rhyme *"i* before *e,* except after *c,* or when sounded as *ay,* as in neighbor or weigh" is a good rule that is easy to remember.

Teachers find many problems in sentence structure. Some pupils are still not careful to begin each sentence with a capital letter and end it with a period, question mark, or exclamation point. Another common problem in sentence structure is called the "comma splice." Here a comma is used instead of a period or a semicolon (;). The result is usually a long clumsy sentence. Often part of the meaning is obscured:

> He can't afford that jewelry, in my opinion, his wife doesn't like it.

What does the writer mean? Does he believe that the jewelry is too dear, or does he believe that the lady doesn't care for it? Or does he believe both? We don't know because the writer failed to give us the information clearly.

Although there are other ways to correct comma splices, the easiest way is to use a period instead of one of the commas. Thus the sentence can be revised in whichever one of these ways best expresses what the writer meant. For example,

> He can't afford that jewelry, in my opinion. His wife doesn't like it. [These sentences mean that the writer thinks the jewelry is too expensive. In addition, he knows that the lady doesn't like it.]
>
> He can't afford that jewelry. In my opinion his wife doesn't like it. [These sentences mean that the writer knows the jewelry is too costly. In addition, he thinks that the lady doesn't like it.]
>
> I believe that he can't afford that jewelry, and that his wife doesn't like it. [Here it is clear that the writer believes that both things are true.]

Some students run sentences together incorrectly by connecting them with words like *and* and *so*. For example,

> Fred dropped the glass and it broke into a million pieces and they went all over the floor so he had to stop and pick them all up so it was a long time before he could get his drink.

This sentence should be divided into a number of shorter ones.

> Fred dropped the glass. It broke into a million pieces, which went all over the floor. He had to stop and pick them all up. As a result, it was a long time before he could get his drink.

Another common problem has to do with selecting the right verb form for the subject of the sentence. The singular form of the verb is used even though the sentence appears to have more than one subject if, when the sentence is carefully considered, it describes each subject acting individually, or only a single subject.

Every Tom, Dick, and Harry is going to be there.
My cousin and loyal friend is coming with me.
["My cousin" and "loyal friend" are really the same person.]
Neither Ted nor Tom was sick.
"Hunger Fighters" is a good book.

If two or more subjects are connected by *but, or,* or *nor,* the verb form can be singular or plural, since the verb must agree with the subject that is closest to it.

Neither they nor I am going to the party.

Collective nouns, such as *crowd, herd, flock,* and the like, should sometimes take a singular verb, and sometimes take a plural verb. When the entire group acts as one, a singular verb is used. When the group does not act as one, a plural verb is used.

The herd was going into the barn.
The herd were going in many directions.

In any case, keep a good grammar book (possibly the student's English text) nearby to resolve troublesome questions.

The vocabulary used in the paper should be simple and direct. Nouns, verbs, and adjectives that are exact and specific are more accurately descriptive than more general words. Meaning is much clearer when we say that an individual was warm, sensitive, and concerned than when we say he was nice or (worse yet) far-out.

Many words are particularly good at conveying sensory messages and really help the reader to see or feel what is being described. A thesaurus and a dictionary can be useful here. The writer should try to avoid words so commonly used by others that they lose their freshness and ability to convey meaning.

It's a good idea to help your youngster learn to proofread. Check his rough copy against the preceding list of common errors. Make a list of the types of errors you find, being sure that the two or three most frequent ones head the list. Explain each kind of error on the list and ask the student to use the list to proofread the paper. If there are many kinds of errors, it may be better to ask him to correct only the two or three most common types. Then the two of you should go over the rough copy together, while you identify and correct the remaining errors. (The student should keep a copy of his proofreading list so that he can use it to check other papers.)

If the teacher specified the characteristics of the title page, the student should be sure that everything requested is there. If no specific demands were made, the title page should include the name of the paper, student, and teacher. The specific class for which this paper was written should be identified. The date of submission of the paper should also be given.

The paper should be neat. Its margins should be straight and at least an inch away from the edges of the paper. At the bottom, the margin should be an inch and a half. Margins (and double-spaced typing) afford the teacher an opportunity to make brief comments on the paper as she reads. There are few things more frustrating for the teacher than wanting to write a comment without being able to find the space for it.

If the paper is handwritten, it should be neatly and clearly done. Leave enough time for frequent rests when it is written, so that the writing doesn't sink into illegibility. When the final copy is written, it should be proofread again most carefully.

Put the completed paper in a protective folder. Good, inexpensive report folders are available at stationery stores. They keep the report itself from getting dog-eared and dirty, and they make the paper a more finished-looking product.

CHAPTER 11

"But he likes to read! He can't have a reading problem!"

You may feel that your child is a good reader because he reads voluntarily. You are astonished when his teacher says he has reading problems. What's going on? Is his voluntary reading limited to easy material for amusement or relaxation? His teacher demands that he read books that are harder for him to understand. If he has comprehension problems, see Chapters 4, 5, 6, and 12.

But it's possible that the teacher has another kind of problem in mind. In school (and outside too), people often have to do something with the information they read—solve a math or science problem, write a report, study for a test. The skills that are used to work with the material *after* we've read it are called study skills. Talk with the teacher and the student. Does the trouble show up in these after-the-reading activities? If so, this chapter will be helpful to you. It describes common study skills problems and tells you how to deal with them.

Dawdling

A common problem that affects people, whether they're honor students or just scraping through, is dawdling. Everything takes more time than it should. Some things get done poorly or not at all as a result. The dawdling aggravates everybody. There are many reasons why dawdling occurs. It can often be helped relatively quickly and easily.

Usually the student sits down, perhaps with two hours of time. He knows he can get his assignment done in less time than that, so he does something else first.

Often the something else gets interesting or takes more time than he thought it would. Maybe a friend calls up, or he has to do an errand for the family. Before he knows it, the time has slipped by, and he suddenly realizes that he no longer has enough time to do a good job on tomorrow's assignment.

If the pupil has the skills he needs but dawdling is still a problem, discuss it when both of you are calm. Point out, as I have done in the last two paragraphs, how the problem sneaks up on people, including yourself if that's the case. Tell your student that you have a suggestion that will be helpful.

The solution is easy, and unbelievably effective. When the pupil sits down to start the assignment, he should estimate how long it will take—let's say an hour—and then work like blazes to finish it within that time. He shouldn't permit any interruptions or do anything else, until the job is over. I find it a great source of satisfaction to gain control of the situation instead of letting it control me—and I get it done a lot faster than when I tell myself, "Oh well, why rush? I've got two hours to do it."

Problems and Solutions in Following Directions

Students have many problems with following directions. When the student misreads directions, either he won't be able to do the assignment or he will do a lot of work only to discover that he has "hit the nail right on the side." That is, he has done another assignment instead of the one he was asked to do.

The student frequently comes to us and says "I don't know what to do." Often he has read the directions too quickly. He has only repeated the words to himself. He doesn't know what to do because he hasn't visualized each of the steps described, which is a slower, more painstaking process. It's useful at this point to ask the youngster to read the directions aloud. In most cases this slower reading enables the student to "catch on," and no further help is necessary.

When rereading doesn't help, we need to know just where the difficulty is. Bear in mind that directions usually give three different kinds of information. The trouble lies in one or more of them. Here are directions in which each of the types of information is labeled:

When two words are combined to form another, the new one is called a "compound word." Below is a list of compound words.	1. *Introductory statement*— identifies the area we'll work in. Provides a key definition in this case.
housewarming highflown journeyman foreword background	2. *Specific material*—to which we will have to do something.
Break each of the above words into two original parts. Define each part. Then define each compound word.	3. *Specific directions*—tell what we are to do with the specific material above

Explain the three different types of information that the directions give. Ask the pupil to find and label each of them in his assignment. This categorizes the information and breaks the larger problem of comprehending the directions into smaller ones. The student should ask himself:

1. What aspect of English (or math, etc.) will I work with? Is there an important definition or explanation here?

2. What words, sentences, examples will I be working with?

3. What am I supposed to do with this material?

If the pupil cannot tell you the answer to one or more of these questions, ask him to read the appropriate part of the directions. The pupil may think he understands it when he doesn't, so ask him to stop at the end of each sentence and say it in his own words. Be especially watchful for words and phrases whose meaning is not known. If the directions say "Give a homonym for each of the underlined words below," the problem may be that he doesn't know the meaning of *homonym*. Look up the word in the student's textbook or in a dictionary, and the problem is solved.

The student may be unable to follow the directions correctly even though all of the words or phrases are clear to him. Then probably he doesn't fully understand the process he is being asked to use. Look at these directions.

We can often make new, useful words by adding suffixes to familiar roots. For example, "quick" (root) plus "ness" (suffix) gives us "quickness". On each line write the new word you get when you combine the two word parts given.

branch + ing ——————————————————————

span + ed ——————————————————————

lazy + ness ——————————————————————

edge + y ——————————————————————

rate + ing ——————————————————————

pace + ing ——————————————————————

trap + ed ——————————————————————

These directions offer no problem when we combine the first pair to form *branching*. However, the other examples can't be combined that easily. The person who wrote the directions assumes that the student knows the rules that demand spelling changes in those circumstances. So in *spanned* and *trapped* the last consonant of the root word is doubled to keep the vowel sound short as in cat. Otherwise, adding the endings produces a vowel-consonant-vowel situation (sp*a*ned, tr*a*ped). This gives the vowel the long $\bar{a}$ sound as in escape.

Where the vowel at the end of the root is long to begin with (r*a*te), we drop the final *e* when a root is added that begins with a vowel. The new word (r*a*ting), still maintains the vowel-consonant-vowel sequence, which keeps the root word's vowel long. Lastly, the final *y* in words such as *lazy* is changed to *i* when a suffix is added (lazinoss) unless that suffix begins with an *i*.

The directions asked the pupil to add a suffix to a root word. The pupil won't do it correctly if he doesn't know the rules that govern that process.

In such instances, the directions are incomplete. You will either have to tell him or teach him the rules that the directions left out. Which will it be? In telling, we just drop the information in the pupil's lap. In teaching, both the pupil and the tutor have to work harder, because we assist him to work the idea out for himself. When people work to learn something, they remember it better than if they passively hear it. So teaching is better than telling. However, there are times when telling is all you can do.

You are working with your youngster, teaching rather than telling. He's getting more and more uncomfortable. Finally he turns to you and says heatedly, "I don't want to know *why* it's done. Can't you just tell me *how* to do it, and save your explanations for later?" That kind of statement is a surefire cure for low blood pressure. However, before you let your hurt feelings lead to angry words and a deteriorating situation, sit back and think for a moment. (You can always yell later, if you want to.) There's a good chance that your youngster said what he did because he's feeling more emotionally squeezed than you are. He may feel that he's not capable of understanding his lesson and may be embarrassed about admitting it. Or, because of other pressures, he may have had it "up to there" at this moment and may be temporarily unable to learn what you're trying to teach him. He may be rejecting your explanations for reasons that have nothing to do with rejecting you, or your feelings about what's important. He can't do the work, and his back is to the wall. How will you react?

The angry, rejecting response he seems to have invited is what he needs least. It won't help him get the assignment done, or feel better about himself, or you. It *will* tell him that you're not in his corner. At this moment he can't learn why the task is done that way. You can indicate your support by showing him what to do, or helping him get the assignment done. That can be a vote of confidence, because you show him that he's worthy of being helped. Please understand that you should not make it a habit to rescue your child every time he's in trouble. That's an awfully good way to teach him that he doesn't have to be responsible for what the world asks him to do. (If you feel your youngster leans too much on the help of others, read Appendix D of this book.) An important part of emergency help is that the two of you will get together soon on another occasion, when the pressure is off, to teach the student what you couldn't teach him when the pressure was on. Nor can the second lesson be extracted as the price for help in the first one. The second lesson takes place because you care about the student, and he needs to learn something that he doesn't know. (Again, see Appendix D if you feel that the student consistently waits for you to pull his chestnuts out of the fire even though he knows how to do the job.)

However, suppose you feel the student will accept the teaching, and you want to try to teach a principle. How do you do it?

Let's take as an example the rule that says that if a word ends with a short vowel followed by one consonant (*can*), that consonant must be doubled before adding an ending that begins with a vowel (*can*ning). Help the student to draw the conclusion to be learned. Ask him to read each of the following lines.

tap	tapped	knot	knotting
pet	petting	rub	rubbed
pin	pinned		

Tell him that the words in the first column have been changed by adding one of two endings in the second column. What are these endings? *(ed* or *ing.)* What do these endings begin with? (A vowel.) What has happened to the last consonant of the root word when an ending that starts with a vowel is added to it? (The last consonant of the root word is doubled.) Now add a third column, alongside the other two, writing the words *taped, Peter, pining, noted, rumor.* What happens to the first vowel sound if the consonant is not doubled and the next letter is a vowel? (The first vowel is pronounced long, or says its name.) If the student can't formulate the rule by himself, write the rule with one or more of its key words left out, and ask him to fill in the blanks. Now see if the youngster can apply the rule by doing the assignment.

Directions with Multiple Tasks

Frequently a set of directions asks a student to do two, three, or more things. Yet many children do only the first thing requested. How can we avoid this common problem? We must teach children that written directions are extremely concentrated. They have to be read much more slowly and carefully than, let's say, the typical novel. When the student reads the directions he should carefully count the number of different activities he is being asked to do. Then he should reread the information that tells him what the first activity is. When he is sure he understands that, he should do that first task, remembering that it is only the first of a series of (perhaps) three. On completing the first task, he should go back and carefully read the directions for the second task, doing it only when he is sure he understands it, and bearing in mind that there is still a third task to be done. Then he should carefully read the directions covering the third part of the job, understand them thoroughly, and do the third task. When he is finished, he should quickly review all directions, to make sure that he has done what the assignment asked.

Textbooks Have Aids to Help You

Modern textbooks contain many aids to assist the students to do their work more efficiently, and with better understanding. If you as a parent are still thinking of the kind of textbook you had in school, look at modern texts. You will be quite impressed with all of the new features available to help the student. However, the student must take time to discover that they are there, and use them.

People are often shortsighted in doing an assignment. They're so anxious to get it over with that they try to do the assignment immediately. They don't stop to see what help the textbook gives, for fear that they will waste a few minutes. Actually this "wasted" time usually helps them to do this and many other assignments more quickly and effectively. I can recall clearly that when I was in the fifth grade I had to find a map that showed the United States in 1820. I remembered seeing some maps near the middle of my book. I went to that section and began turning pages in an effort to find the right map. It was an aggravating, inefficient, unsuccessful process. Accidentally, I later discovered that the page right after the table of contents named each of the book's maps, together with its page number. Inefficiency does more than lead to aggravation. Sometimes it wastes so much time and energy that we give up the task in disgust either without having done it as well as we could, or without having been able to do it at all. For all of these reasons, it really pays to get acquainted with the helping devices offered in a textbook.

The best time to look at the special aids in a book is at the very beginning of the term. If the book is examined before the first assignment is given, the student won't feel that this delays his getting to work. Then too, the earlier he sees the book's helpful features, the larger number of assignments he can do utilizing their aid. In addition, the first time he sees the book he is more curious about exploring it than he will be later. If the term has already begun, giving the book a once-over will still be valuable. In addition, as specific assignments come up, it's good to spend a few minutes looking to see if the book has study aids that can be useful. It often does.

What should the student look for when he first examines a book? The title page contains very little information, but all of it can be important. It gives the data the student needs for footnotes if the book provides information for a paper. The title page may also give some information about the author's knowledge of his subject. The back of the title page tells the copyright date. This date is usually two or three years after the author wrote the book. In areas such as current history and science, new information comes in almost daily, but nothing that occurred even a few years before the copyright date is likely to appear in the book. Of course the book will not discuss anything that occurred after the last copyright date either.

Almost every textbook has a preface. It may contain useful information such as the author's approach to or fundamental beliefs about his subject. It may specify the particular audience for whom he wrote, or give other useful information.

Table of Contents

A careful look at the table of contents before reading the book is almost always extremely helpful. I say "almost," because in a few cases, the chapter and section titles are so general as to have no meaning until after the text is read. Whether it's read before or after, the table of contents gives an overview of the material to be covered. After all, it was the plan by which the author wrote the book, and is the structural skeleton of the book. Following this analogy further, each bone is the main idea that is connected to other main ideas with which it has a common function, much like the bone groups that form arms or legs. Each of these groups is connected, again like a skeleton, to form the framework of a complete organism (or in this case, a body of knowledge). No one can really understand the meaning and function of an arm unless he sees its relation to a body. No one can understand the meaning and function of a chapter unless he sees its relation to the book. In that sense, nothing else in the book shows the reader so clearly what the author had in mind. Nothing else explains as well why these specific ideas were put together in this sequence. Properly used, a good table of contents is an invaluable study aid.

Those who use the table of contents only to find out what page a given chapter starts with have disregarded its most important use. The table of contents relieves us of the necessity to decide which of the book's ideas are details and which are the much more significant main ideas, because the table of contents lists only main ideas. It lists all of them, in a sequence that shows their relationship to one another. If we don't use the table in this way to see the structure of the book, we have two alternatives. We can read the book and figure out this structure for ourselves, more or less reproducing the table as though it had not been done already. Or, we can read the book without discovering its structure. In that case we see only unrelated bits and pieces, none of them apparently more significant than the others. We have failed to grasp a major part of the book. What we have grasped we will not retain, since unrelated material fades quickly from memory.

Directly after the table of contents many books have a page or pages that list maps, graphs, charts, and tables, or special illustrations, with their page numbers. While we don't need these lists for every assignment, when we do need them we can only use them if we know they exist. Since they can save us a lot of time and effort, it's worth knowing they are there.

The Appendix

At the back of many texts and other books you will find an appendix or appendices. Their contents are related to the nature of the book in which they're found, so what they tell us varies widely from book to book. A how-to book's appendix may tell you where to order the supplies and tools the author mentioned previously. A social studies book's appendix may include important documents in the history of a country. There may be few times when you need this information, but often when you need it, you need it badly. If you have not examined your textbook to see what help it offers, you may have to spend hours to locate that information elsewhere. There are few things more frustrating than doing that and then finding out later that the information was readily available in your text.

The Index

After the appendices comes another great saver of time and work, the index. Its nature is often confused with that of the table of contents, but they are very different. The table of contents is a "map"—it shows the book's major ideas in the sequence in which they are discussed. It locates these ideas by giving you the number of the first page that discusses them.

The index also lists ideas and gives you their page numbers. However, the index stresses details rather than main ideas. If you want to know where a specific person, place, or thing is mentioned in a book, look it up in the index; the table of contents won't tell you. The items in the index are arranged in alphabetical order, not in the order in which they appear in the book. The index doesn't explain or integrate ideas. It locates them for you.

Although the basic principles of index construction are the same from book to book, the finer points are not. For example, an index entry "cotton gin" may list three page numbers, each in a different kind of print. In one book, boldface type tells on what page the object is defined. Italicized type indicates a diagram showing how the machine works. Normal type signals a table, chart, or map. The student who knows what kind of information each typeface indicates can save time in assignment after assignment by going directly to the page he needs. To find out what the different typefaces mean, he should look at the beginning of the index. There he will probably find a key or legend that tells the function of each typeface. If not, it's easy to figure out the key. The student should look at three index entries that have page numbers in the same typeface and see how those pages deal with their subject entries. For example, if each one has a definition, he knows what that typeface stands for. He uses the same technique for the other typefaces.

Using an index is a simple process. Sometimes, however, we can't locate a specific topic in it, even though we know that the information is in the book. It's in the index somewhere, but we haven't found the right entry word. How can we find it? First, we try to think of a synonym for the word. If there is nothing listed under "gasoline" we try "fuel," "fossil fuel," "oil," "petroleum." If that doesn't help, we try to think of other key words in the situation, even though they aren't synonyms. If the student wants to know something about the *Clermont* but there is no entry for it, he should look up "steamboat," "Fulton, Robert," etc. (Robert Fulton's steamboat was the *Clermont.*) Perhaps the topic he seeks is discussed as one of a number of items under another heading. If he wants to know something about oil in Texas, and has found nothing under "oil" or any of its synonyms, he should look up "Texas." There may be several subheadings under Texas. (Any Texan will tell you that the information about Texas could never fit under just one heading.) If so, one of them will probably deal with Texas's oil.

If the student still can't find what he wants, he should look in another book, or ask another student in the class how he got the information. There is one other thing he can do if he is desperate: take a quick look at the table of contents. Although locating specific details is not the job that it was designed to do, the table of contents may give him an idea of where to locate the information—but he shouldn't bank on it.

The Glossary

Many textbooks contain a glossary, which is usually located at the back of the book. The glossary is an alphabetical list of the book's technical words, with the meaning of each word as it is used in that book. The word probably has other meanings too, but the glossary rarely gives them. That's one great advantage of using a glossary: It tells exactly what the author means when he uses a word. A dictionary can give fifty or more definitions of a word. The reader must decide which one his text's author really meant. The glossary gives only the right one for that book.

The glossary has another great advantage too. The reader who is stumped for a word doesn't have to put his book down and pick up a dictionary, which may be across the room, to get help. It's all conveniently there, and exactly right.

The glossary has other advantages. The reader can use it to study for a test of that text's vocabulary. He can also use it to locate quickly the definition of a word he's not sure of. However, the student can only get help from a glossary if he knows it's there and uses it.

Charts, Graphs, Tables, and Maps

Charts, graphs, and tables appear in just about every textbook. They are almost universally disregarded by readers. When I gave a class a quiz on a completed reading assignment, I often asked them for information that was presented in those visual aids but nowhere else in the text. Very few students answered correctly. Many pupils were resentful, and others felt I had asked an unfair question. They seemed to be saying, "If you had told us, we would have paid attention to these figures, but we don't ordinarily." Yet authors and editors consider visual aids an efficient way to present information. Why don't pupils pay attention to them?

Pupils have learned that many illustrations (especially paintings and drawings) really don't say anything new or valuable. In fact, some are put in only because the editor feels that otherwise the book will look too imposing and difficult to read.

Sometimes the author makes an important point with a table or chart. That point belongs right after a specific paragraph. But when the book is set in type, that paragraph ends too close to the bottom of the page; so the visual aid is placed elsewhere, after some other paragraph, to which it is not really connected. So it's tempting to generalize from experiences like these and to conclude that none of the visual aids says anything important.

In any case the pupils were told to *read*. In their minds that's a very different process from looking at pictures and diagrams. Then too, looking at charts and graphs doesn't appeal to those of us who get anxious when we deal with mathematics.

Yet these visual aids often do make points not otherwise dealt with in the text. But first we must look at and understand them.

Visual aids have no value by themselves. The author presents his ideas in a sensible order, A, B, C, D. When one of these ideas, let's say C, is presented via a visual aid, the reader should try to understand it after B and before D. However, as we have seen, the book doesn't always print it in that order. Grasping C's meaning before B or after D damages the sequence and sense of the author's argument.

Assuming that the visual aid in question does contribute significantly to the reader's understanding, how can the reader grasp what it tells him if its message is not immediately apparent? There are two choices here. Some people try to discover the fundamental point of the chart (graph, table, etc.) by learning what its details say, relating these details to each other and then deciding the principle of the whole thing. A better alternative is to work in the opposite sequence. First we look at the title of the chart to determine its fundamental thrust. If it has no title, we can often get the same information from what the author says just before or after the visual aid. In either case, we must first find the visual aid's major point.

Knowing its major point in advance is a great help in examining the chart because it eliminates many possibilities when we try to figure out what its details say. If the chart's title is "U.S. Agricultural Production, 1940–1950," we have a pretty good idea of the products that will and will not appear in it. We also know what time period will be covered, and which nation's production is involved. If we had no title, or disregarded it, it would take us a lot more time and effort to get the same information.

We can get a general idea of a visual aid's purpose by seeing what kind of aid it is. In the same way, when we see what tool a carpenter uses, we know something about his immediate task. If he's using a hammer, he's probably driving nails. If he's using a saw, he's cutting something. An author uses visual aids as his tools. He uses a pie or circle chart to show what proportions something is divided into. The pie starts with 100 percent of something, say the federal budget, and shows what proportion of it went into different spending categories. A bar graph can be used for the same purpose. It can also compare the relative popularity of several competing products in one time period, or how production of one product rose or fell over a longer time period.

A line graph is a bit more complex. It can show how one item's production or one set of scores changes over a given time period. Other kinds of lines can be drawn on the same graph. If each of those lines symbolizes another product or set of scores, the chart can show a clear picture of how each product or score varied as time went on, and how all of them varied with regard to each other.

A flow chart is an illustration that is often used. It shows a process that has many steps. Each step is illustrated or labeled and has arrows leading to and away from it. The flow chart shows all the steps in a given process, and the sequence in which they are done.

The tree chart looks like a tree, but is used to show family or other relationships. This chart may start with the earliest members of the family at the bottom and "grow" up, or it may start at the top and "grow" down.

A map is a symbolic description of the earth, or part of it. It looks as though it were drawn by someone sitting high up in the sky, copying the earth below. Of course, since the earth is round, when the mapmaker (or cartographer) draws on a flat surface, his work can't be as accurate as when he is drawing on a globe.

The statistical table looks much more forbidding and difficult to read than a line graph, because it consists of columns and rows of figures. It gives the same kind of information, however, as a line graph: It shows how a series of products or set of scores vary with regard to time and to each other. The main difference is that the table gives exact figures, which a line graph rarely does. A table can state that 562,846 cars were produced, but a line graph may have to represent that figure as a dot (or a line) roughly halfway between the indicators for 500,000 and 600,-000. On the other hand, the line chart much more quickly and dramatically shows the relationships between the figures involved. The author usually chooses the kind of visual aid that best makes the point he wants made.

No matter which visual aid is used, the student should use the following procedure to get the most out of it. First, he should decide at what point this visual aid belongs in the author's sequence of ideas, and study it there. (It may already be there.) Second, by looking at its title and the text that surrounds it, he should get clearly in mind the point that this aid makes. In doing this he should also consider what type of aid it is, and what that type is usually used for, as seen in the previous paragraphs. Third, he should study the aid to see what it shows. If it uses symbols, the first thing to do is learn their meaning. Is there a key or legend? It will tell the reader what each symbol used means. If there is no key, he should look at the aid's labels. The axes of a line graph, the columns of a table, the critical parts of any visual aid must be labeled to be meaningful. Before the student tries to see what the message of the aid is, he must understand the labels, because they tell him what kinds of information are presented.

The pie or circle chart is probably easiest to understand. In the example below, the title says that its purpose is to show what products the Jones Motor Company produced last year. Each piece of the pie has a name and a percentage. For example, one piece says "Cars 60%." It means 60 percent of the units they made were cars. The proportion of the circle shown for cars is exactly the same as the proportion of cars in their total production. If we compare the size of the different wedges, we can see clearly what proportion of their production went to each type of vehicle.

JONES MOTOR COMPANY PRODUCTION—1978

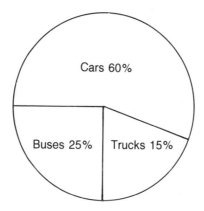

The bar graph isn't difficult to read.

U.S. CAR PRODUCTION—1970

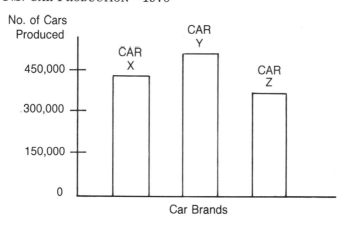

Bar graphs have two edges, one at the left side and one at the bottom. They are called "axes" (plural of "axis"). Look at the axis at the left of the graph. It (generally) tells how many units were produced, or sold. It is marked off like a ruler. When the bars to the right of it are vertical, the higher the bar is, the larger the quantity it represents. The bottom axis is labeled "Car Brands." Because we've looked at the title we know that the graph is talking about the U.S. production of cars in 1970. This production will be compared by brands, rather than by engine size or any other basis. To find out how many brand Y cars were produced, go up to the left axis until you reach the height of the top of the column showing brand Y's production. That height clearly represents 450,000 cars. Brand X's height falls halfway between the markings for 300,-000 and 450,000 cars. The distance between those two markings represents 150,000 cars (450,000 minus 300,000 equals 150,000). Half that distance represents half of 150,000, or 75,-000. Since Brand X exceeded 300,000 by 75,000, it produced 375,000 cars.

The line graph can look quite complicated but is really simple to understand.

RELATIVE POPULARITY OF THREE COLA DRINKS, 1970–1975

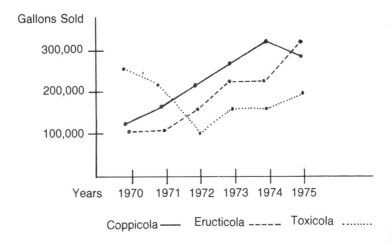

The graph's title tells us that it will compare the popularity of three cola drinks in the years 1970–1975. The legend names the three brands for us and demonstrates how each brand will be identified on the graph. The left axis tells us that its figures represent gallons sold. The bottom axis indicates the specific years in which the sales are counted.

The line graph gives us a great deal of information. It tells which drink was most popular in each year, and which was least popular. It shows which drink had the greatest increase in popularity, and which had the greatest decrease. Much more information can be found in this graph.

Flow charts and family tree charts are relatively easy to read. The flow chart's sequence of activities is almost always quite clear. However, the chart will not be meaningful unless the reader knows at least the purpose served by each of its steps. Of course if the reader also knows just how each step accomplishes its purpose, so much the better, but this is not always possible if the processes are too technical.

Maps are complete mysteries to many, and valuable sources of information to others who are no more intelligent. Those who use maps successfully (probably the same is true for all the other visual aids), are people who relax and are not threatened when dealing with them.

There are many different types of maps. They may show weather, industrial or agricultural products, political subdivisions, population density, land features, and many other things. The title and the legend or key should be studied first. Often a map tells us where north is. The map-reader should stop and think of the area as though it were on a globe. He should see this area's relationship to north and south, its placement, and its size in relation to the rest of the world. Then he should examine what the map tells him, and should try to fit this into its place in the author's line of argument.

Tables of figures often appear in texts. Again, those who take a relaxed attitude toward them will learn more. The table's title and its relationship to the headings found in the columns and rows will be helpful. The table's numbers don't show increases and decreases as dramatically as the line or bar graphs do, so it's up to the reader to think about them as though they were displayed in those ways. He should look at each column or row of figures to see what trends (increases, decreases, etc.) are shown for each product. That gives him a rough idea of the trends that each of the products displays with regard to each other. Now he can see what specific information the author took from the table, and where it fits into his line of reasoning.

No matter which visual aid the reader sees, he should ask himself five questions about it:

1. What kind of information does this type of visual aid usually convey?

2. What facts and figures does this aid present?

3. What is the fundamental conclusion that these facts and figures illustrate?

4. What function does this conclusion have in the author's reasoning? (Be sure you put this conclusion into the proper sequence in that reasoning. That's not necessarily where it's located in the book.)

5. What additional information can be drawn from the information directly presented?

In any case, it's important to relax and learn how to get the information that visual aids offer. Those who do that get more out of their reading. Those who don't, get less. Each visual aid that is not understood can poke a hole in the reader's understanding of the book.

Working effectively with one book can demand the use of many different reading and study skills. The student who is competent in some of them may need help in using others. After all, nobody is equally able in all the things he does.

CHAPTER 12

"I studied,
but I failed the test."

The student who says he failed even though he studied may be excusing himself, but a great deal more than that is happening to him. If he spent a reasonable amount of time studying, he's scared and he's hurt because he tried and he just wasn't good enough. You may feel that he doesn't care, but aren't there other reasons for failing too? If he doesn't care, why did he study at all? Have you ever tried to do anything that you were supposed to do, without caring about how you performed? If you failed, how did it feel? No, I think very few people really don't care. When they have failed a number of times they *act* as if they don't care, so that their hurt won't be visible to others. They may feel so hopeless that they stop trying. But they hurt, and they *do* care.

I'm interested in *how* this youngster studied. Did he fail because he wasn't studying effectively? If so, this book can help you to change that.

We can learn how to study a book effectively by seeing how the author writes one. First the author selects a subject. That subject consists of a number of major areas, which the book must describe. For example, Book A's subject is the administration of a particular U.S. president. It must discuss the state of the nation when he became president, the national and international problems during his term in office, what was done about them, and the consequences of those actions. Each of these areas is discussed in detail, sometimes in several chapters. The trouble is that often the details take on a significance of their own. That is, the student reads and studies the details as though they themselves were important, although actually they are only important as parts of that president's administration. The student has lost sight of the fundamental purpose of both the book and the section of it that he is reading.

Thus many students make no attempt to grasp the author's outline as they read. Instead they search through the book, alert only to pick up those individual facts that may be needed as replies to short-answer questions. Almost all of the work the author has done to organize and present his ideas is lost to them. Why?

Pupils read in that way for a number of reasons. Often they are afraid they lack the time or ability to read the book in a way that they feel is more demanding or time-consuming. It seems easier to memorize details than to figure out the outline of the book, to see the relationship of those details to the outline, and only then to memorize the details. Besides, many of the exams they take seem to stress the ability to memorize unrelated details rather than digest organized bodies of information.

Essay vs. Short-Answer Questions

Years ago, almost all the tests given, except those in math and science classes, used essay questions exclusively. These questions explored the students' understanding of central currents and trends in the material they studied. They showed if the student could tell the difference between details and more important ideas, and how the student organized them in his thinking. Only after he organized the subject matter in this way could he think critically about it, if he wished to.

However, studies showed that essay questions were marked very inconsistently. Teachers in the same department showed wide variations in the grades they gave any one essay. In fact, marking essay questions fairly is very difficult to do, and quite time-consuming. It took little to convince many teachers to drop essays and switch to objective, short-answer questions. The only thing objective about them is the way they're marked, since each student's answers are compared to the same answer key. The teacher's feelings about that student don't enter into the marking of the test. Hence the scoring is objective, quick, and convenient. Although short-answer questions *can* tap the student's knowledge of the author's reasoning, such questions are much harder to make up than those that ask for details. Then too, students regard the more thought-provoking questions as difficult and unfair, if they are not used to them. On the other hand, the teacher certainly needs to see if the students have learned the details. For many reasons then, many teachers rely primarily or exclusively on short-answer questions. These tend to emphasize the memorization of details, rather than the ability to organize knowledge or think critically about it.

Often students read or study a text in accordance with the kinds of questions they expect to be asked. They look only for sentences that can easily be turned into short-answer questions. This approach theoretically brings good marks. It looks easier than trying to grasp the author's conceptual framework. Is it effective in producing good marks? Here's how to find out quickly.

How Can Your Student Learn More Effectively?

This experiment takes only a few minutes and demonstrates a very important point, so please try it. You will need this book, a pencil and paper, a watch with a second hand, and a friend. It would be good if the other person doing the experiment was the student you were trying to help. This is designed to show which of the two methods of learning we've been talking about is best.

1. Turn to Appendix A, page 219 of this book. That page is almost completely blank. Put the book face down, without looking at the next page.

2. When the timer says "start" the student turns the book over and opens it to the next page.

3. He tries to memorize as much of it as he can, until the timer stops him after exactly sixty seconds.

4. Then the page is covered, and the student writes as many of that page's words as he can remember.

5. He puts the pencil and paper away.

6. He turns to the next page of Appendix A and gets exactly sixty seconds to memorize as much of it as he can.

7. Then he uses the pencil to write as many of the second list's words as he can.

When he finishes, he counts the number of words he was able to recall correctly by checking the answers against the appropriate printed page. If you haven't looked at or heard any of the words, you should try this experiment too, using another sheet of paper. When you both finish, come back to this page in the text. (It might be a good idea to read the directions over, in order to make sure that they are clear in your mind before you start. When they are, go to it.)

Now that you've done the experiment, your results are probably consistent with what occurs each time I do the experiment in my classes. Nine out of ten people do better on the second, categorized list than they do on the first, uncategorized list. Typically, they remember about twenty-two items from the first list, and about thirty-three from the second, or half again as many. Only about one in ten students remembers more from the uncategorized list than from the categorized one. It always turns out these people categorized the first list while trying to memorize it. The experiment proves two things: (1) Information is easier to recall when it is categorized, that is, when the student sees the relationships that bind it together. (2) If the student categorizes the material himself, he remembers it better than if it is categorized for him.

You may have noticed that only the second list had a heading. It was my way of telling you that all of the categories below it actually were part of one larger category, "Food and Drink." People who remembered that title got a lot of help, because it suggested the other categories below it. These categories in turn suggested their own component parts.

Thus we see that even those who only want to memorize bits and pieces for short-answer exams can profit by recognizing the subject of the book and its various major topics. This approach categorizes the information and connects the categories to each other. Students who read that way will understand and remember more information, and for a longer period too.

Sometimes even good students feel that if they understand the individual statements that appear in their reading, they have mastered the material and don't need to study it anymore. That just isn't true. They haven't learned the material unless they can close the book and reconstruct what it said, which demands that they have fully understood and *organized* their reading.

Survey Q3R—How to Study So You Won't Forget It Tomorrow

Over the years, scientists have carried out many experiments that tell us how to comprehend more effectively, and how to remember what we've comprehended. Francis Robinson has put together a method, Survey Q3R, that incorporates many of their discoveries. SQ3R is for the reader who has to read a chapter of a text or study it for a test.

Survey. With practice, this process should take about a minute, says Robinson. The student looks at the chapter title and all the headings in the chapter. He also reads the chapter's first and last paragraphs, which usually introduce and summarize what has been said. The object is to see what major topic the chapter discusses, and to learn what areas that topic is divided into. There are usually about three to five such areas.

Question. Each of these areas usually has a heading. Take the first heading, and turn it into a question. For example, if the heading is "The Causes of the Civil War," your question becomes "What were the causes of the Civil War?" This must be a broad question, instead of the short-answer type, because the information needed to answer it is spread over several pages in the chapter. It brings to mind what the reader already knows about it. More important, it gives the reader a purpose for the next step.

Read. Now the student reads this section. His express purpose is to gather the information that will enable him to answer the question. As he reads, he writes a few brief, headlinelike phrases that list only the main ideas and the most important details presented. Outline form clearly shows the relative importance of each.

Recite. When he has finished reading the section, he presumably can answer the question he asked himself. He closes the book and sees if he can answer from memory. If he can't do it, or isn't sure, he can look at his notes or the book to check. When the student is satisfied that he knows the material, he makes up a question for each of the remaining sections of the chapter in turn, and then reads and recites to see if he can answer it.

Review. When all the sections of the chapter have been covered, the student looks over his notes to reinforce his knowledge of them. Further, this enables him to see again how all the parts of the chapter are related to each other. Robinson suggests that the student should review by covering his notes to see if he can recite the most important headings. Then each of these should be uncovered, while the student tries to remember the less important points under each one. However it is done, this review is extremely important in fixing the material in the student's mind, as we shall see.

Actually each of the steps in Survey Q3R is the result of investigations into how people learn and retain and what they read. Why survey the material? Experiments show that a survey is quite helpful. In one instance, students who were taught to preview read the material in 24 percent less time than non-previewers, with no loss in understanding. Obviously, the minute or two spent in surveying saves time, even though it appears otherwise.

Why ask a question before reading a section? Clearly, a good question gives the reader a purpose and tells him what to look for. This helps him to differentiate between more and less important information. A question based on a section title also makes him conscious of this area as part of the author's line of reasoning or presentation. In reading to answer the question, he looks for the most relevant information and integrates it into the author's thought pattern. Without such a question, students often do no more than read "to find out what it says," in some vague way. It's comparable to the difference between looking through a book of craft projects with no purpose in mind and looking through it because we want to make a stool, and then finding exactly the information we wanted. We are more involved and take more away from the book in the latter instance. Further, experiments show that students who are given questions before they read have better comprehension of the material (and remember it longer) than students who read it without questions.

As for the brief notes (in outline form) that the student writes to answer the question, again experiments confirm that even students who have had less than two months practice in making these notes comprehend far more of the material than similar groups that do not take such notes.

In the third step, review, the student closes his book and tries to answer aloud the question he used to guide his reading of the section. How well does his answer correspond to the notes he made in step two? The recitation gives him practice in presenting the material to others, which he has to do in school. And repeating the material shortly after it is learned helps the student to remember it. A large-scale study showed that high school students tested immediately after reading something remembered an average of 53 percent of it. After two weeks, they recalled an average of less than 11 percent of it. A group who reviewed the material one day after reading it remembered 46 percent two weeks later. A group who reviewed the material right after reading it recalled 83 percent of it one week later. Unfortunately, this latter group was not tested two weeks later. However, it is clear that reviewing the material shortly after it is learned is the most efficient way to decrease the forgetting that takes place. Experiments also show that students who write things down with the awareness that they will have to repeat them, remember them far better than those students who write them without such awareness and, obviously, better than students who don't write them at all. Further, experiments also tell us that students who review the material in a series of short periods of time remember it better than students who spend the same amount of time reviewing it in one long period.

SQ3R is a powerful tool, because it incorporates much of what we know scientifically about how people learn and remember. As is the case with most worthwhile things a person does, it isn't done as effectively or quickly the first few times the student tries it as it will be when he's had some practice.

Outlining

There is another way to help the student who seems to understand what he is reading, but can't say what he has learned when he finishes the assignment. That is to teach him to outline properly. Both SQ3R and good outlining demand that a pupil grasp the fundamental outline (or conceptual structure) of the author's presentation, so they have a great deal in common. When should the pupil use one rather than the other?

SQ3R can be used to teach a pupil how to read in order to find an author's thought pattern or organization of material. It is also very useful if a pupil has to master a limited amount of material, say one or two chapters, for a test in the immediate future. If done as Robinson suggested, however, the pupil's notes will usually be too brief to be really helpful if he has to study them for a test more than a few days after he reads the book.

Outlining, on the other hand, should be used by the reader who already knows how to discover the organizational pattern of the material. If such a reader needs to prepare the material for a test or a report a week or more after he reads it, he will need to use an outline. If he has to master the material in a whole book or a few books for a test, he will be better off if he outlines the text(s).

Outlining is a powerful, valuable tool. To do it well, the student actively searches for the outline from which the author wrote the book. He must identify in turn the main topic, its major subdivisions, and supporting data. This forces the student to become actively involved in learning, which in itself, as we have demonstrated, causes the material to be remembered better. The act of writing itself also reinforces learning. Lastly, the person who studies a good outline has a great deal less to do than the person who studies the much longer text, and at little sacrifice in the material covered.

Perhaps the pupil is reading material now which he will need later for a midterm or final exam. Perhaps he is collecting material for a report. In any case, to be most useful, his outline of what he has read should have the following characteristics:

CHARACTERISTICS OF A GOOD OUTLINE

I. It must be relatively brief.

   A. Brevity means that the outline should use abbreviations and meaningful phrases instead of longer sentences.

   B. Brevity also means that some of the details and illustrative examples mentioned in the text must be omitted.

II. The outline should clearly indicate the conceptual skeleton of the material read.

A. A title should clearly state the main topic so that the student knows what he is responsible to learn. Will he learn how to catch a trout, or how George Washington felt about foreign affairs?

B. The outline should clearly show that the main topic is divided into a number of subtopics (or main ideas). These subtopics are:

1. Each of about equal importance.

2. Of less importance than the main topic, since each subtopic is only a part of it.

C. Each subtopic should clearly be supported by details. In turn, these details are:

1. Each of about equal importance.

2. Of less importance than the subtopic, since each detail is only a part of it.

Each idea's position on the page shows its importance. (Knowing this will also help you get more out of other people's outlines.) The main topic, the most important idea in the outline, is indicated by the title. The title's importance is shown by the fact that each of its words starts with a capital letter. Further, it is the statement that comes first, ahead of the others. The importance of the remaining ideas of the outline is shown by their distance from the left-hand margin. The closer the idea is to the margin, the more important it is. All subtopics start at the margin. The more important details used to support them should start about an inch farther to the right. Less important details should start still another inch farther to the right. Each group of details should be listed directly under the idea it supports or explains.

Thus an outline is a shorter version of information originally presented elsewhere. It is written to show at a glance the author's fundamental line of reasoning. The reader can immediately see the main topic, its major subdivisions, and their supporting details. All of these are neatly categorized by the out line. Further, it quickly shows the reader the relative importance of each of the ideas presented, and which ideas are of approximately equal importance. Unlike a steak, a well-done outline is rare. But it is worth learning to do.

Can your student do a good outline? If you're not sure, turn to Appendix B, which contains a brief, well-organized article. Ask your student to outline it, and then compare his outline to the one in Appendix C. (Don't let him see Appendix C beforehand, of course.) It's important to see if the pupil starts to write his outline almost as soon as he starts to read the text. If he does, the outline will probably be unsatisfactory. The student should first look the article over to see what topic he is responsible to learn, before taking notes. That topic should be a clear, accurate statement written as the title of the outline. It needn't necessarily be exactly the same title the author gave it. Sometimes the new title is clearer and more useful to the student than the title of the article.

If you feel the student's outline can be improved, but aren't sure of what's wrong with it, turn to Appendix C. Here you will find a poor outline with its errors clearly labeled. You will probably find the same kinds of errors here as your student has made.

One point is important. When you help someone to outline, you may run across spelling errors. Deal with them later if you wish, but not during the outlining lesson. Most students find it hard enough to work with one goal at a time. It's much harder to deal with two. This also means that if the outline has several areas that can be improved, you can't work on them all at the same time.

The techniques of SQ3R and outlining are of use primarily to students who are relatively competent. Students who have trouble with understanding and recalling the meaning of easy sentences, or with accurately grasping main ideas, will have to solve these problems first.

CHAPTER 13

"If you thought the other questions were hard—"

Sometimes the student has to answer a question that stumps him. In trying to help, you may find that the earlier parts of this book don't cover the problem. That is, the question requires an answer that does more than give details, main ideas, or the author's line of reasoning. Here are some examples:

1. Compare and contrast the programs of two political leaders or parties in a specific election.

2. Describe the personalities of the people in a specific book, story, or article.

3. What program would you suggest to the president to help solve the nation's energy (or other) problem? Explain why you make each of your suggestions.

4. Should the United States impose a higher tariff against foreign steel (or take some other specific action)? Explain your answer in detail.

5. Someone recently stated a lengthy opinion on a given topic. Evaluate the ideas he expressed.

Why are these questions (and others like them) so hard? They ask the student to evaluate, add to, and reorganize information in accordance with his own beliefs. Just evaluating alone is hard. It asks the student to decide if the information offered is true, complete, and relevant, and if the author's line of reasoning is correct. Don't you sometimes feel uneasy when you do these things?

Some students are uncomfortable unless they can check their answers in the text. They can't do that with this kind of question, since the student's thinking won't be in the text. Some students don't trust their own judgment or ability to make decisions, and feel that this kind of question will reveal their weaknesses. Other students lack the kinds of skills necessary to answer these questions, because these skills are learned through experience and they haven't had many questions of this sort.

Evaluative questions often deal with controversial topics. You have your own opinions on those, which increases the opportunities for conflict between you and your student. While it's always important that you establish a good teaching atmosphere, it's especially important to maintain one when you are working with controversial assignments.

A Good Teaching Atmosphere

The responsibility for a good teaching atmosphere is primarily yours, not the student's. And it's a big responsibility too, particularly because this is not a meeting of equals. One of you is older and much more experienced than the other. If the two of you are parent and child, remember that there are many adults who are real achievers but don't feel that they're adequate people, because they never got that message from their parents.

The student's earlier feelings of dependency upon and respect for you are always present. Even though your advice is not always taken (which is probably as it should be), your attitudes and opinions about the worth of the younger person have tremendous impact. It's up to you to determine whether that impact will be supportive or destructive. After all, when you "competed" against this child in board games and physical activities when he was younger, you were careful to lose on some occasions and win on others. The game itself was not as important as the welfare of the other person. You wanted him to feel good about himself so that he would continue to develop and to try. Are these goals less important now because you're concerned with evaluative thinking instead of playing games?

What can you do to create an atmosphere of respect that encourages growth? You should demonstrate acceptance of the student. That doesn't mean that you must pretend that whatever the student says is right. It means that you behave in ways that show that you respect him and value his right to have and express opinions, even when those opinions oppose yours. Further, as the more mature person, you should be careful to limit your comments to the merits of the issue itself, and should not give in to the temptation to blow off steam by commenting negatively about the student's intelligence, honesty, or ability to think clearly. These comments don't clarify the issue under discussion. Worse yet, they tell the listener that you don't respect him, an opinion that is even more wounding because of your greater authority. When one of two people who are concerned about one another is stronger than the other, the stronger one should see to it that his advantage is not used unfairly. So disagree when you feel you should, but limit your comments to the issue.

Sometimes the opposite situation occurs. You want to compliment the student for something done well. Again, limit your comments to describing the issue. It's better to talk about how hard the task was, or how apt the solution was (if these are true), than it is to generalize by saying that the student must be brilliant, or is always correct. One student said to me: "I feel as though I'm choking when my parents praise me and tell me that I'm a genius. I know I'm not that good, and that I won't be able to live up to what they think of me." In praise or criticism, talk only about the task and how the person might have felt when he did it. Dr. Chaim Ginott's book *Between*

Parent & Child is very good at illustrating many such comments, and describing their effects on the listener.

Respecting the other person also means respecting his opinion though it differs from yours. You don't teach people to respect evaluative thinking and reading when your primary concern is converting them to your own point of view. You teach evaluative reading and thinking when you emphasize the logical tightness and factual soundness of both their position and your own, and that's not an easy thing to do. It's particularly hard to (1) realize that some arguments that support your position are false, and reject them; and (2) realize that some arguments that oppose your position are true, and accept them.

There is still another issue. In practice you usually oppose X's position because of its weaknesses and support your own because of its strengths. But in life it's impossible to find issues in which all the weaknesses obligingly line themselves up on one side, while all the strengths obligingly line themselves up on the other. Making good evaluative decisions, of both the kind that teachers sometimes ask for, and the kind citizens have to make, depends on the ability to say, "I see the strengths and weaknesses of both sides clearly. One side, however, fits my interests better than the others."

One last point. You should serve as a good example by refusing to hold opinions so tightly that you can't change your mind when new evidence tells you that you're wrong. After all, many times we have to make decisions without knowing all the facts. On some issues all the information isn't available, even if we want to look it up. So inside, a small voice ought to say, "This is the best decision I can make—for now. I may have to change it someday."

Answering Compare-and-Contrast Questions

Relatively little evaluation is demanded in "compare-and-contrast" questions. They do demand more work than other types of questions, and there is a specific way to do them. First, the student should be sure to reread the question so that he has it clearly in mind. He should gather the materials that tell him the position that each side takes. *The New York Times Index* and the *Reader's Guide to Periodical Literature* are at the local library. They provide a good reference source for information on current topics, the subject of most questions of this sort. The student should take notes on cards as discussed in Chapter 10. It's a good idea to use one color for Side A's cards and another color for Side B's, so that the student can tell them apart easily. The research process tentatively ends when he thinks he has enough information to describe the viewpoint of each side, a point usually reached when the new information coming in only duplicates what he already has. He should then lay out the cards that describe one side's position in a long straight line on the left side of a large table and, without piling one card on another, arrange the cards into groups. For example, the cards on international affairs might go at the top part of the line, and the cards on domestic affairs at the bottom. Within each category, he should arrange the cards in sensible order, putting cards that deal with the same specific topic close to each other. In the next step the student takes the cards that describe the second viewpoint and puts them on the right side of the table, being sure to place cards that discuss the same specific topic opposite each other. He should check the card arrangement for completeness. Does he have statements that tell only how one side feels about something? Is the information he has a complete statement of each side's views? He should try to get whatever information is missing.

When the lineups are complete, he should look at the point of view of the two sides and try to characterize each side. Is one more logical, more liberal, more farmer-oriented, etc., than the other? If so, he should make this point in his introduction, which he can now begin to write. He then describes each of the topics on which the two sides agree. Mention of each of the other topics follows, with indication of the contrasting views held by each side. The student can conclude his answer to a "compare-and-contrast" question with a brief statement that cites the similarities and differences in a general way. It should be consistent with, but should not simply repeat, his introductory paragraph(s).

Characterizing Literary Figures

First, as always, the student should make sure that he understands the question clearly. A question that asks for characterization implies an answer that has certain specific attributes. The physical characteristics of the person are often relatively unimportant, unless they are unusual or affect the person's life deeply. A characterization question usually demands more emphasis on the important aspects of someone's personality. What ideas are important to him or her? How does this person deal with other people? What do the goals of his life tell us about his interests and values? How does he respond to frustration and discouragement? Does the person change significantly in the book or story? How bright is he? How honest? These and other questions can be considered.

The student starts by gathering information on index cards, even though he may not be quite sure what this information's significance will be. No matter if he later decides not to use some of it, he must gather enough to be able to draw conclusions. What information should he look for? He should try to find situations in which the person to be characterized solves problems. Solving problems usually involves making choices, and the things a person chooses to do and the ways in which he does them reveal the things that are important to him. The student should be sure that the cards include the central problem faced by the character in the book or article, and what he or she did about it. If it's important, he should include a card that describes the person physically.

Now he should read the cards over and sort them into rough categories such as "Attitudes toward Friends," "Major Goals," "Honesty," or whatever categories come to mind. Next he should read the cards in each category again. If a card describes information that belongs in another category as well as this one, he should write it on another card and file it in the other category too. If a card is in the wrong category, he should put it where it belongs. Cards that describe one personality trait that is seen in different incidents belong in the same category. The student should not attribute a characteristic to someone if it is only revealed in one incident, unless that incident was a very important event. Then he makes a pile of cards for each personality attribute he's found. Is there enough evidence to support his conclusion about the existence of each personality attribute? Has he identified enough of the attributes presented by this character? If the answer to either or both of these questions is no, he should go back into the text and get more evidence.

When he has enough evidence, he arranges the piles of cards in the sequence in which he wants to describe the person's attributes. The sequence should reflect some logical approach. Perhaps the student can discuss the character's attitudes toward himself in one category, and his attitudes to others in another, for example. The student should begin his paper with an introduction that gives a general opinion about the person's character. It should make the reader curious to find out why he wrote what he did. Perhaps the student could say that he'd welcome X as a neighbor enthusiastically, or he could say that if the character bought the house next to his, he'd move to Europe. The body of the answer, which describes characteristics and shows the evidence that led the student to decide on each of them, follows next. Then he needs a summary statement that reflects his introduction but doesn't repeat it. Perhaps he can tell why he would have liked to have known X, or how X's personality shaped his accomplishments.

Discussing a Program Designed to Solve a Problem

First, as usual, the student should make sure that the assignment is understood clearly before any work is done on it. It's far too easy to answer the wrong question.

PRESENT THE PROBLEM

The student is being asked to discuss solutions for a particular social problem, so it makes sense to describe the problem itself first. He should discuss its importance and as much of its nature as the reader will need to know to understand the solution(s) under discussion. He will include the problem's important parts and the conflicting interests of those involved in it. The textbook may provide some of this information and will suggest other materials that do. (See Chapter 10 on reports, for additional sources of information.) However, the student should spend only about 10 percent of his paper discussing the problem. The paper's major thrust should be the solution(s) and his evaluation of it (or them).

PRESENT THE SOLUTION(S)

How he presents the solution(s) depends on what he has been asked to do. If he has been asked to evaluate one solution, he should locate that one. If he must provide his own solution, he is expected to locate and read the suggestions of several experts to help him decide how he would solve the problem. In either case, he must now locate the information he needs. His textbooks may be helpful again, but he may need more up-to-date material than they have. At the library, the previously suggested *The New York Times Index* and the *Reader's Guide to Periodical Literature* are good references for current affairs. The student's local reference librarian will have other sources if he needs them.

If he is evaluating one solution, he should note its main ideas and details on index cards. He should aim for accuracy and get enough information so that he won't have to go back to the library to check on or fill in something he missed.

Producing his own solution requires more work. He should read and note on index cards what typical experts have said, making sure, as always, that the upper-right-hand corner of the index card states the specific topic discussed. Each card should indicate the source of the information (in case he has to go back to it again) and the viewpoint presented.

The information the student collects should come from people with different points of view. If he is trying to suggest a program that will solve our energy problems, for example, he should be sure to read the opinions of both industry and consumer representatives. Also, if possible he should read the ideas of neutral people—government officials, investigative reporters, or university authorities, although these people often speak from a particular point of view too.

As he collects opinions, the student will notice that the same topics come up again and again. For example, if the subject is energy programs, he will probably find repeated comments on conserving energy by limiting the use of it, the development of new types of energy, encouraging a life-style that uses less energy, and encouraging more energy production through legislation that would decontrol prices and offer tax incentives for exploring new energy resources.

If he is evaluating only one opinion, he should arrange his index cards according to the various topics they deal with. Then he should put the topics in the order in which he plans to describe them, since describing them is the next step.

If he is evaluating several opinions, he should arrange his cards on a big tabletop so that he can see the information he's collected very graphically. Cards for each topic ("Tax Incentives," "Saving Fuel," etc.) should be set down in a straight line on the left side of the table, with plenty of space left between them. Across the top of the table, the student puts out cards labeled "Industry Views," "Consumer Views," "Other Views." Now he takes the cards on which he's written the opinions of the experts on those topics and arranges them in their proper place on the table, lining them up in the correct rows according to topic and in the correct columns according to the source of the opinion.

Now he inspects his cards. Does he have all the solutions that have been suggested? Does he have information on each side's reaction to every solution? If he has gaps, he will have to do more research or his paper won't be complete.

The student should use the tabletop arrangement to help him describe these opinions when he writes his paper. He can do this in one of two ways—either describe what is in each column, telling first what one group believes about each of these solutions, and then what each of the other groups believes in turn; or describe what is in each row. In this case, he takes each suggested solution and tells what each of the opposing sides says about it. He should make sure to use only one of these approaches in describing the opinions of the interested parties. His paper will then be well-organized and is likely to get a good grade whether the reader agrees with him or not.

EVALUATING THE SOLUTIONS

Whether the task was to evaluate someone else's program or to develop one of his own, the student must evaluate the opinions he's gathered. This process has a few steps.

EXPERTS, OTHER EXPERTS, AND NONEXPERTS

The student must first evaluate the writers of the statements he read. Either the articles themselves will tell him or the library can help him find out what training, expertise, and jobs these people have. Do they really know a lot about the subject? An expert's opinion is likely to be supported by facts and more carefully thought through than a nonexpert's opinion. However, the student shouldn't be intimidated by the expert's status. He should feel free to disagree when he thinks he should. After all, experts disagree with each other too, so they can't all be right. Is this person's job in the community likely to affect his point of view? He may sincerely believe that what's best for the producer (or consumer) is what's best for the country. If the student disagrees with that belief, he may not like that expert's other suggestions either.

There is a danger here. It's awfully tempting to accept or reject what an authority says strictly because of our feelings about the group he represents. There's something to be said for that when there isn't any other basis on which to decide. But when we can explore the question ourselves, why give up the right to make up our own minds?

For that matter, experts aren't the only ones who have good ideas. In any case, the best thinking sometimes is blind to the source of an idea. If it's true it's true no matter who says it.

EVALUATING THE FACTS, SO-SO FACTS, AND NOT-SO FACTS

Facts carry a lot of weight in an argument. Whether we like them or not, they can't be wished away. We have to ask ourselves, are the facts presented in a line of reasoning really true? That's no great problem, because facts can usually be verified at the local library. Both sides of a dispute ought to be able to agree on what the basic facts are. However, are all the relevant facts being presented? For example, when an advertisement states that 75 percent of all the doctors asked preferred aspirin to relieve pain, that's probably a fact, but there may be other relevant facts too. Did they ask twenty doctors, or two thousand? Were these doctors employed by an aspirin company? What kind of pain were they talking about? Then too, many products are basically aspirin, but have something added. Did these doctors prefer one of these products to others?

To find out if all the relevant facts are being presented, the student should see what the opposing viewpoint says about his topic. If he reads many points of view, he's much more likely to get all the relevant facts than if he reads only one.

Some pieces of information only look like facts. They are really opinions. Opinions are easy to recognize when the writer uses a phrase such as "I think," "I believe," "It seems that." If the student is trying to decide whether a statement is a fact or an opinion, he should remember that a fact can be verified elsewhere, but an opinion cannot. Clearly, facts are better evidence than opinions are. An opinion is a statement that says that since someone has been unable to prove that something is true, he can only believe or hope that it is.

However, statements shouldn't be discarded altogether just because they are opinions. Each must be examined carefully. For example, an expert's opinion about something in his own field is more likely to deserve our consideration and respect than the opinion of someone who knows little about this field. If an expert's opinion agrees with one that is held by people who otherwise oppose his view, we're inclined to feel that the opinion is valid.

EVALUATING THE LOGIC

What about the reasoning in the experts' statements? As a statement goes from one point to another, the student should look carefully at the logic that connects them. Are these two points really connected to each other the way the author says they are? Could they be connected in some other relationship? For example, when two things happen at about the same time, we often feel that one is the cause of the other, particularly if that seems to make sense. However, we used to think that people got malaria because they breathed gases that came from swamps. After all, people who lived near swamps got malaria, while those who lived away from swamps did not. It all seemed quite logical. Now we know that they got malaria because infected mosquitoes who lived in the swamps bit them. So we must examine the reasoning and be careful with what appears to be true if it has not yet been proved to be true.

Are the writer's emotions influencing us too much? It's appropriate to make some decisions without using logic. Whether I order chocolate or vanilla ice cream, when they're both of equal cost and food value, is strictly a matter of which one I like more. But some questions demand a response based at least partly on reason. Often, however, people sway our decisions on these issues in purely emotional ways. Our best defense against this is to recognize these attempts for what they are.

They take different forms. One consists of simply attaching emotionally weighted words to the idea under discussion. Commercials never referred to "Jell-O," but only to "delicious Jell-

O." A former prominent federal official identified certain political programs as those of "effete liberals." Whether or not you think Jell-O tastes good depends on your own reactions to it, not on someone else's opinion. In the same way, whether or not you favor a given political program should depend on your reactions to it, not on someone's assertion about the sexual preferences of the people said to favor those ideas.

Another technique seeks to sell a product or program by making a link between it and something else we all feel positively about. A bumper sticker I saw recently said: "Keep America Strong! Build Your House of Stone!" All of us want to keep America strong, of course, but there is no real connection between that and the material we use to build our houses.

Still another technique uses testimonials. Even an unpaid testimonial by the beautiful Mademoiselle Frou-Frou about her use of Glitsch Beauty Cream is nothing more than a suggestion that it *might* be helpful to other women. And a paid testimonial can easily strain the honesty of the person who does the recommending.

Two related techniques ask us to favor an idea or a candidate for similar reasons. In one technique, the candidate who asks our support for himself or for something he favors because he's one of us—just "plain folks". We generally like people who are like ourselves. However, that's really irrelevant compared to what he or his program really offers. When Adlai Stevenson ran for president, a picture of him showing a hole in the sole of his shoe was widely reprinted. Possibly some of the editors who used it felt that it would show that he was just an ordinary person like the rest of us. That reasoning always makes me uncomfortable. I think the president should be more capable than the rest of us. Humorously, I found myself wondering if we ought to entrust the leadership of the nation to someone who couldn't keep his own shoes soled.

The other technique asks us to support someone or something because "everybody's doing it." Using that theory, Edison would never have invented the electric light, since everybody else was using candles or lamps that burned oil or gas. In any case, how many people support the candidate is relatively unimportant. What he stands for is the real issue.

"Card-stacking" is a technique that selects or falsifies the evidence in order to convince us of someone's point of view. An alert, questioning attitude, together with a willingness to look things up (including what other people are saying about it) are the best antidotes for this one.

It's important to examine all arguments carefully. The reader must remain alert. If he doesn't use evaluative abilities, no one will use them for him. It's a good idea to ask yourself, "If I agree with this writer's (or speaker's) assumptions and think he has used all the relevant facts, are these conclusions inescapable, or at least quite probable?"

EVALUATION AND OUR BIASES

Everybody has biases—likes or dislikes that are not reasonable, but which still affect his decisions. There isn't a great deal we can do to rid ourselves of them, but when we know what our biases are, we often can prevent them from pushing us in the wrong direction. If a student knows he has unreasonable feelings about something, he has to be especially careful not to let himself be too swayed by those feelings.

Sometimes you or a student takes a position and continues to defend it long after it's clear that the position is indefensible. Maybe bias is involved, but maybe not. Someone may have a bias, but can't do anything about it if he doesn't recognize it. Or, either one of you may have reasons for maintaining your position that you're not aware of, reasons that have nothing to do with the issue under debate. If you can't figure out what's going on, back off, since there is no point in continuing to hammer away.

DRAWING OUR OWN CONCLUSIONS

The student is now aware of the size and scope of the original problem, the viewpoint and competence of those who wrote about it, the accuracy and completeness of their information, the validity of their logic, and the possible effects of the student's own biases on his opinion. He is now ready to decide how the problem should be solved. He can tell what he thinks of each of the solutions offered and why he thinks that way.

Once in a while it's acceptable and sometimes even desirable to say that we can't take a stand on a specific idea, because in spite of our efforts to find it, there just isn't enough information. A no-stand decision should be used as rarely as possible, and should not prevent the student from doing what the assignment asks, which is either to suggest a program to solve a problem, or to evaluate somebody else's solution.

Answering an evaluative question is an exacting process. The student should not expect to rush through it or be surprised if it takes more time and effort than answering other kinds of questions. It should. It's a valuable process to learn, because it's useful in many of the difficult decisions we make as citizens.

In reading their students' answers to questions like these, teachers don't expect to find superb solutions. They want to see if their pupils are aware of the solutions that are being suggested, and they want to see some evidence that their pupils have thought carefully about them.

CHAPTER 14

In conclusion

We've come a long way together since the beginning of this book. I'm sure that you now know a lot more about what your youngster's reading and learning difficulties are, and how he or she feels about them. You also know more about how you can help. By now, most of you have done some work with your children. If this has been a new experience for you, you've learned something positive. You've learned how to help, and your child has learned how to be a better student. Both of you feel good about the improvement, and about working out the problem together.

Some families haven't been that lucky. You've tried to help, but to no avail. Maybe you can't be patient enough because of outside pressures (and there are always plenty of those). Maybe your child is too uncomfortable about revealing his weaknesses to his parents. That's not easy to do. For whatever reason, it hasn't worked. You and your youngster may be feeling guilty, angry, and inadequate. But you are now actually closer to solving the problem than you ever were before. You now know that one solution won't work, and that you should consider other possibilities. Many other things can be done to help. Appendix D, page 229, "I've tried, but—" tells you what they are.

Most parents who use the information this book gives them with time and patience can succeed. Some parents come into my office with their backs to the wall. They are desperate. Sometimes they are angry and they condemn everybody—their youngster, the schools, their spouse, themselves. When parents learn what is really going on, and how to be helpful, they start to feel better. Their negative attitudes change, and they become more relaxed. The effort and good will they bring to bear often result in substantial improvement.

Three Who Are Succeeding

Here are some examples of youngsters whose parents have learned how to help.

Bruce is a tousle-haired tenth-grader. He generally looks a little sheepish and moves slowly. His teachers reported that his comprehension and knowledge of vocabulary were weak. Understandably, he also had considerable difficulty in dealing with evaluation questions. He overemphasized the importance of speed and felt that people who read rapidly had to be reading well and accomplishing a great deal. He was very concerned about his own poor academic performance.

His parents and he worked together for a few months. His teachers and parents agree that he is now considerably more accurate in identifying main ideas. He monitors his reading to see if it makes sense, although he didn't do that before. He needs much less help in dealing with evaluation questions. His rate of reading in social studies has gone from 175 to 235 words per minute, although he hasn't done any work specifically designed to increase his reading speed. Last term his grades placed him near the bottom of his class, but he is now much closer to the middle of it. His parents are continuing to work with him.

Mike and Ronda are eleventh-graders. Mike is middle-sized, good in sports, and a little wary about revealing that he doesn't know something. Ronda is short, dark-haired, and pretty, but quite intense. She's even prettier when she's relaxed and animated. They're in the same school. They were given achievement tests at the end of the last school year. Their parents worked with them for a few months. Then the school gave them another form of the same achievement test.

Originally, Mike was weak in comprehension and study skills. He was motivated and persistent, but found it difficult to use good study methods and to organize his work, especially long-range tasks such as term papers. He was global and vague rather than precise and accurate in dealing with main ideas and details. His comprehension and vocabulary scores are stated below in percentiles. For example, his comprehension score was 34 before he worked with his parents. That means that his comprehension was no better than that of the bottom 34 percent of the children in his grade across the country.

	Comprehension	Vocabulary	Rate
Before	34	55	195 wpm
After	63	69	226

He is continuing to work with his parents, who feel he has made progress, but still needs to become more precise in the way he grasps ideas. He also should become more flexible in reading rate, since he tends to use much the same pace no matter how difficult or easy the material is.

Ronda was overly careful. She read far too slowly and was weak in vocabulary. Here are her "before and after" percentile scores and reading rates.

	Comprehension	Vocabulary	Rate
Before	20	14	50 wpm
After	39	44	143

Ronda needed work in comprehension. She is now much better in dealing with main ideas. As a result, she understands more clearly what each paragraph is about, and how its ideas are connected to the paragraphs around it. Her parents have helped her to be more alert to the words whose meanings she doesn't know. She now figures them out or looks them up, using their meanings to help her understand the sentences in which she found them. As a result, her comprehension has improved. Because she understands more quickly, her reading speed has tripled, though no other effort has been made to improve it. Her test scores are better because her comprehension is better, and because the resultant increase in reading speed enables her to answer more questions during timed tests. She now spends less time doing her homework and completes a much larger portion of her work during class time. Her parents are continuing to work with her.

When Your Child Learns, but Doesn't Carry It Over

A common problem is that the youngster learns new techniques in the work with his parents, but doesn't use them when he's working without their supervision. This problem is usually temporary, but let's talk about it.

There are probably three major reasons why newly learned techniques are slow to be used. Some people see the new technique with a kind of tunnel vision. They work so hard to learn the technique that they forget that it's a tool to be used to study something else. So they don't think about applying it elsewhere.

Another reason why it takes a while for students to use the new techniques they've learned also explains why they are often slow to learn the new technique. Kids don't get to be the way they are overnight and, like the rest of us, they can't change rapidly. Even if the technique they have been using all along is not very effective, it's like an old shoe—familiar and comfortable. It's hard to abandon something you know for something you don't know or are just learning.

A third reason has to do with tension. When a person isn't sure of himself and tense, he is likely to use older, more familiar techniques rather than newer ones he's not as sure of.

Whatever the cause of the failure to carry over, expect the problem to occur. Its solution is relatively easy. Remind him of the situations in which the new technique can be used. Check up from time to time, to make sure that the youngster uses it with appropriate assignments. Be patient and supportive when you do this. Increasing the tension in your student only makes it harder for him to use the new technique. The problem will disappear soon.

How Will You Know that Your Child Is Improving?

That isn't a silly question. Learning and carry-over are often slow. How can you tell if your work is bearing fruit?

You shouldn't try to answer that question until at least several weeks or two months have passed from the time that you began to help. First of all, you and your youngster have to get used to the new situation. After that, the youngster learns what you are trying to teach. Still later, he beings to use what you've taught him in doing his schoolwork. So don't expect instant improvement.

However, after a while you will see changes—signs that good things are happening. Possibly his notebook will be more organized, and the notes in it will improve. Past-due and undone assignments should decrease. Your student will show more involvement with his schoolwork. There will be fewer skipped classes and unauthorized absences, if these have been problems. The youngster may be more comfortable in going to school. He may make the time to do his work, without your having to remind him while he delays and delays. And of course, in time you should begin to see a slow but steady improvement in his marks. The nicest changes, however, don't concern schoolwork directly.

There should be less friction and more good feeling between you and your youngster. If you work well with him, you will begin to tune in more and more to the difficulties he faces, and to the ways he deals with them. That should help you to have more appreciation for the kind of person he is. On the other hand, he will see that you're firmly behind him, not only with good feeling and acceptance, but also with the kind of meaningful help he needs. Your youngster will feel better about you but, more important, he will feel better about himself. There is nothing quite like being able to say, "I see myself defeating a problem that I couldn't defeat before. I'm growing more capable. I feel better about myself." If this is what you have helped your youngster to do, congratulations. The whole struggle has been worth it. I hope you realize just how great a contribution you have made to the life of your child.

Appendices

APPENDIX A

Two Brief Learning Tests

plate	circle
Ford	level
drum	saucer
brown	Pontiac
France	pencil
pen	triangle
square	red
pliers	saxophone
cup	Italy
Plymouth	chalk
crayon	platter
ellipse	purple
hammer	Greece
Germany	Buick
paper	cello
green	wrench
viol	rectangle
drill	bowl
Austria	Chevrolet
trumpet	yellow

Food and Drink

beef	potatoes	wheat	apples
lamb	spinach	oats	oranges
pork	peas	rye	pears
veal	carrots	barley	cherries
chicken	broccoli	corn	grapes
bourbon	milk	sugar	pie
brandy	water	salt	Jello
gin	soda	pepper	chocolate pudding
Scotch	coffee	cinnamon	ice cream
vodka	tea	cloves	ices

APPENDIX B

An Essay to Outline

Coal—The Burning Issue

Our ever-increasing use of oil is a matter of major concern. We are rapidly depleting the world's reserves of oil. Further, we depend upon foreign nations for much of the oil we use. These nations can at any time limit what they sell us, or raise its price steeply, as they have done in the recent past.

It is no wonder then that we are presently planning to reduce our consumption of oil by increasing our use of coal. Vast reserves of coal exist within our own borders. It is clear that when we convert large numbers of oil-burning factories and power generators to the use of coal, we decrease our dependency upon oil. Desirable as this is, we should be aware that the increased use of coal will bring other consequences that are negative and potentially serious.

Coal miners and their families will be the first to feel some of the negative results. Since 1900, over 1,100,000 miners have either lost their lives or been crippled permanently in mine accidents. The dreaded "black lung disease" has made invalids of an even larger number of miners. At the present rate, it is estimated that the government will soon be paying close to $10 billion a year in pensions to black lung victims.

The rest of the nation also faces health risks, though they are somewhat less dramatic and immediate. The burning of coal releases dangerous substances into the air we breathe. Some of these are poisonous, others are radioactive, and still others produce cancer. Another chemical in smoke is a primary component of smog, which is already a problem in some of our large cities. Sulfur dioxide is also released in smoke. It is an important factor in causing some common, fatal respiratory diseases. It is also a factor in other diseases that don't kill their victims directly, but weaken their general health so that they get other fatal diseases.

Another threat to our health comes from the fact that coal smoke contaminates the air with tiny particles of solid matter. These particles are too small to be trapped by the smoke filtration devices in smokestacks. Because they are so small, we breathe them into our lungs, which contain many tiny passages. These can become blocked by accumulations of the coal smoke particles. Further, there is some evidence that these particles also cause cancer.

A sharply increased use of coal, such as the government currently plans, would also change many of the conditions that exist on earth now. While some of these changes might be good, others have the potential for great harm. Thus one of the chemicals released in the burning of coal is carbon dioxide. Scientists are concerned that enough of it can be released into the atmosphere to raise the earth's temperature and alter our weather in other ways as yet unknown. Raising the earth's temperature would require us to burn less fuel for heating, but might substantially affect how much food we can produce, among other things. These are issues that can become serious problems.

Another example of environmental damage due to the use of coal is seen in the increasing acidity of rain. This has already decreased the growth of our plants and trees. Further, animals and plants that live in bodies of fresh water are also hurt by it. This same acidity partially removes chemicals from our topsoil, further reducing our crops. The burning of coal also releases other gases into the air that further limit plant growth and health.

Lastly the production and use of coal affects the surface of the earth on which we live. Strip mining has made almost 500,000 acres of our land useless. Much of this land cannot be restored for farm use under the present economic conditions. The poisons in the water found in coal mines have so far contaminated close to 7,000 miles of our waterways. These waterways can no longer be fished. The poisons in them have contaminated many wells.

Our past history shows that coal is very useful, but is not an unmixed blessing. Our present efforts to double the amount of coal we use may help solve one problem, while presenting us with a whole host of others.

APPENDIX C

Two Outlines

Good Outline

What Dangers Come from Increased Use of Coal?

I. Health threats to coal miners and their families
   A. Since 1900, coal mining killed or crippled 1,100,000 +.
   B. Black lung disease strikes a larger no. than that.
      1. Soon government will pay $10 billion a year in pensions to black lung victims.

II. Health threats to all
   A. Chemicals in coal smoke are poisonous, radioactive, cancer-causing.
   B. Another chemical causes smog.
   C. Sulfur dioxide (in smoke) causes fatal diseases.
      1. Also causes other weakening diseases.
   D. Tiny coal smoke particles block our breathing passages may cause cancer.

III. Climate changes
   A. Carbon dioxide (in coal smoke) increases temperature of earth, affecting food production patterns
   B. Higher acidity of rainwater
      1. Stunts growth of plants (food)
      2. Decreases plant, animal life in fresh water
      3. Removes soil nutrients needed by crops
   C. Other coal smoke gases cut plant size and health

IV. Coal mining affects earth's surface
   A. Strip mining ruined almost ½ million acres in U.S.
      1. Much of this not economically restorable
   B. Mine water seepage poisons almost 7,000 miles of waterways
      1. Fish in these now killed
      2. Many wells also poisoned

V. Conclusion: Present plans to double coal production may relieve oil problems, but may cause other serious problems.

Comments on Good Outline

A good title in question form helps the reader know what information he must find.

Five Roman numerals, at equal distance from left margin, tell there are five main ideas of roughly equal importance.

A, B, C, etc. items grouped under the main idea they support or illustrate. Placement farther away from left margin shows these are less important than main ideas.

1, 2, 3, etc. items grouped under the detail they support or illustrate. Placement still farther away from left margin shows they are less important than the details above them. Notes briefly but accurately describe information from text.

PoorOutline

I. We plan to use more coal to decrease our use of oil.

II. However the increased use of coal may bring its own problems.

III. Effects on coal miners and their families.

IV. Effects on nation.

V. Smog
   A. Dangerous drugs
   B. Temperature gets warmer.

VI. Rainwater
   A. Soil ruined
   B. Less acid in rainwater

COMMENTS ON POOR OUTLINE

No title. What is the student supposed to learn? "Coal" would be too general to be useful. "The Poisons in Coal Smoke" is incomplete because it leaves out climate and earth surface changes.

Items **I.** and **II** needn't be written in complete sentences. They can also be combined into one concluding item. See other outline.

Items **III** and **IV** are too general to pass the "Two Weeks Later Test." That is, they are too brief to be meaningful a week or two later. They should mention the death, injuries, and illness suffered directly and indirectly as a result of mining.

V. and **VI.** are really details, not main ideas. Like all the items from III. down, they are too brief to be meaningful.

Items **V. A.** and **B.** are not details that support **V.,** Smog; but are connected to other ideas. In addition, **VI. B.** is not correct. These notes are inaccurate, poorly organized, and practically useless in helping the student remember the text.

APPENDIX D

"I've tried, but—"

A small number of you have tried to help your youngsters, but are discouraged. (If at all possible, work for at least a few weeks, rather than a lesson or two, before drawing the conclusion that your efforts are in vain. What looks like an uncomfortable situation in the first lessons often improves substantially in a short time.) Perhaps you're concerned because you have seen little or no change in the way the youngster works in the tutoring sessions and at school. Perhaps your efforts were met with a failure to cooperate, or produced a lot of discomfort in your student or you. Should you stop the tutoring? If you do, is there something else you can do to help?

What's Going On?

One reason for lack of progress is that the youngster is just not ready to use the help that you offer, even though he needs it badly. Even if you are the kindest, most sensitive person in the world, maybe your student just can't give reasonably good attention and effort to the work, sometimes for reasons that have nothing to do with you. What are the signs of this difficulty?

The youngster's attention constantly wanders away from the work. He looks at the clock frequently and asks how much more he will have to do. He interrupts the work repeatedly to do other things or tries to change the topic of conversation. He can be physically restless, with his foot jiggling occasionally or constantly. He drops pencils, loses the place or the page repeatedly, and often is missing the things he needs for the work. He sits at the edge of the chair, as though poised to flee, throughout the lesson. Or he leans or tilts all the way back in the chair, away from the work, with his body as close to horizontal as it can be. (Don't take any of these signs seriously if they stop soon after the lesson begins. Anxiety is usually at its highest then, but is only a source of concern if it continues throughout the lesson.)

Or, when he works, he goes through the motions, but back-pedals away from the task. That is, he works quickly, doing the job without real thought and effort. Is he doing the assignment too rapidly, to spend as little time as possible in the discomfort of doing it? Perhaps he answers questions before or just after you finish asking them, when he hasn't yet had time to think. Then he usually unintentionally gives the wrong answers, although the questions are easy, and you know he knows better. Sometimes there is a long delay after you ask a question, but then he gives you a wrong answer. He seems to have guessed, because he could no longer stand the strain of doing the problem. Try calmly describing the youngster's pattern to him, and point out how it affects his work. Observe if there is any change in the next few weeks.

If improvement doesn't occur, it's clear that the youngster can't solve the problems, probably because he just isn't comfortable enough to use his ability to solve them.

Or maybe your patience is wearing thin as you see that the hours of labor that the two of you spend produce little positive benefit. Perhaps as a result you are bribing, criticizing, arguing, or punishing during the tutoring, even though you know such methods are undesirable. They prevent the student from feeling good about himself, relaxing, and giving full attention to the school problem that faces him.

Should You Stop Tutoring?

If, after a few months during which neither of you enjoy and look forward to the tutoring, it looks as if the situation will continue, then you should stop your tutoring. That doesn't mean that you're an uncaring parent. There are many other ways for you to help your child.

What Else Can You Do to Help?

You may be asking yourself: Does something else lie behind the learning problem? Does your youngster need help that is beyond what his school or your tutoring assistance can supply?

To help you answer these questions, sometimes you can get useful suggestions from people you respect who have had similar problems, and who have dealt with them successfully—but do be careful. The more specific these friends get, the less likely they are to be describing problems that are similar to yours. The causes of learning and personality problems vary so much from person to person that specific advice from friends about solutions is rarely correct. You are better off with a careful diagnostic evaluation by an expert. Therefore your friends' advice about where to go for help will probably be more useful than their advice about what to say or do to solve the problem yourself.

Talk to your youngster's teachers and guidance counselor. They can be good sources of information. Asking them for their impressions of your youngster's problem and what you might do about it is likely to be easier and more productive if you think about your own reactions to people who talk to you. You prefer people who are calm and reasonable, who don't blame you or others for their troubles, and who assume you are honest and conscientious. You prefer people who don't feel negatively about you just because you belong to some occupational or other group. You hope the other person will be prepared to give careful consideration to the advice he has asked for. In a word, you want to be treated fairly. You resent it when you're not. Why shouldn't the people you talk to want to be treated the same way?

When you describe your problem to the people at school, try to be a reporter—do it as accurately and factually as you can. When you've done that, listen to their impressions of what's going on. Do they think you are expecting more than the student's potential will permit him to deliver?

Sometimes the school recommends remedial sessions or private tutoring. The school can often suggest the names of excellent tutors. They can sometimes be very helpful. Sometimes the school suggests psychological testing, to determine what the youngster's potential ability to learn is, and what, if anything, is keeping him from using it adequately. Ask what facilities are available to help explore the issue. Go to the best sources you can find.

One good bet in such cases is to consider university clinics. They are less expensive than private sources of help. Usually their staffs are well-trained, carefully supervised, and competent. University clinics have another advantage. Their employees' income is not directly tied to whether or not they persaude you to bring your child to their clinic, so they will be quite honest with you. Some reading clinics, such as the one I head, use a diagnostic team, which routinely explores academic, intellectual, and psychological issues. Thus, if the youngster has other problems that interfere with his functioning in school, these are described to the parent and sensible solutions are suggested.

So, if your own direct efforts haven't had the results you hoped for, there are a number of other things you can do. Your youngster will see you trying to help, and will know you are concerned and working to help him. Inside, he will be strengthened by it. Don't give up. Most situations can be improved. Good luck!

Index